PRAISE FOR

CHRIST, CULTURE, AND CINEMA

How do entertainment trends and the biblical narrative relate to each other? Jeffrey Skopak has masterfully crafted an answer. By connecting selected stories from the big screen with the saving stories of Jesus, Skopak interprets Hollywood with God's Holy Word. And since movies also serve as a metaphor for the relationship between theology and culture, we gain unsugarcoated insights into related topics like the power of social media, the cult of superstardom, and the scourge of societal racism. Skopak lays bare both the contemporary significance and the eternal considerations we can and should draw from motion pictures.

Rev. Dr. John Arthur Nunes
Pastor, author, educator, and speaker

Jeff Skopak has put together a delightful study and presents in a very relatable way how the movies can, and often do, influence our faith life, complete with a discussion guide. Drawing on popular and celebrated movies, the book takes readers on a journey of insight and enjoyment as we look at movies in light of culture from a new perspective. It is the marriage of how we can use means like our modern culture as reflected in the movies and gain deeper spiritual insights, all as a platform to connect people to Jesus. This creative presentation reminds us of how our God can use all things, even the things often corrupted by sin, for His glory.

Rev. Dr. Gregory S. Walton
President, The Florida-Georgia District of The Lutheran Church—Missouri Synod

---

CHRIST, CULTURE, *and* CINEMA

HOW FAITH AND FILMS INTERSECT

JEFFREY SKOPAK

CONCORDIA PUBLISHING HOUSE · SAINT LOUIS

Published by Concordia Publishing House
3558 S. Jefferson Avenue, St. Louis, MO 63118-3968
1-800-325-3040 • cph.org

Manufactured in the United States of America

1 2 3 4 5 6 7 8 9 10 31 30 29 28 27 26 25 24 23 22

To my dear wife, Amy, who willingly puts up with my overanalysis of movies and is still willing to watch them with me . . . over and over and over again.

CONTENTS

FOREWORD

Lights! Camera! Action!

When we hear the director of a movie shout this phrase, we know things are really happening, and we eagerly anticipate the outcome. Who knows? Such a production may end up on the silver screen, or at least on our TVs or tablets.

Movies play a significant role in our lives. They permeate our culture. Not surprisingly, they impact the life of the Church too. That is the focus of this book. While this volume doesn't examine movie production, it does explore the meaning and application of familiar movies and how they reflect, either closely or more distantly, biblical themes and principles. To put it a little differently, this book explores how movies affect us, especially as members of the Body of Christ. It also suggests ways in which we might legitimately and faithfully apply their lessons.

Our guide on this celluloid journey is the Rev. Dr. Jeffrey Skopak, a long-time pastor and movie lover. Currently serving at Grace Lutheran Church and School in Jacksonville, Florida, Pastor Skopak brings years of pastoral experience and innovative practice in ministry to his task of understanding and applying the lessons of a wide variety of movies—some well-known and some less so, some very recent and some a bit older. All of the movies treated here share a pointed message that Pastor Skopak successfully unpacks. What's more, he applies the lessons of these movies to our lives as we seek to be faithful disciples of Christ and to reach out with the Gospel to our communities.

In the late 1960s, the *Lutheran Witness Reporter* ran a column titled "Flick Chart," which reviewed contemporary movies. Some people loved the column; others were critical due to some of the movies that were reviewed. Today it remains challenging for us as God's people to decide what is appropriate for viewing and what is not. Some films aren't worth watching, and frankly, others shouldn't be watched. Still, many movies may be watched, and among those, some may provide us with helpful avenues to discuss weighty themes with friends and family who might otherwise be reluctant to engage in theological conversation.

It is in addressing this last category that Pastor Skopak succeeds so well. He offers a distinctively biblical and Lutheran approach to the movies he engages, one that is Christological, incarnational, sacramental, and missional. His careful and insightful treatment of common human joys and sorrows always points us in the end to the promise of salvation we have in Christ. Pastor Skopak's invitational approach lends this book to sharing with family and friends who are in the Church and also with those whom we hope will join with us in the future.

So prepare yourself for a captivating expedition. The characters, themes, and life lessons that emerge throughout this book will change you. And I can assure you of this: you will never watch a movie the same way again!

Lawrence R. Rast Jr.
President, Concordia Theological Seminary
Fort Wayne, Indiana

DARKEN THE THEATER

I love movies! There, I said it! And I suspect, if you have picked up this book and started to read it, you love movies too. There is nothing quite like the anticipation, buildup, and waiting for a big-screen release. The possibilities running through your mind are endless. What actors and actresses will be in the cast? What will the music be like? What costumes, sets, and locations will be used by the director to bring the story to life? And the computer-generated imagery (CGI)! What spectacular things will I see, feel, and experience with this much-anticipated movie?

There is a magical quality about going to the movies—the smell of popcorn, the darkened theater, the seemingly endless parade of previews to tantalize your imagination about upcoming features. And then it happens. The lights go completely dark. Words appear across the screen: "And now, the Feature Presentation—and don't forget to silence your cell phone!" The reason you left the comfort of your home, purchased your ticket, and overpaid for a bucket of buttery popcorn is about to begin.

Movies are reviewed, critiqued, judged, and celebrated, and the lucky few are awarded. The very best of the best cinematic presentations take on a life of their own and are transported to the smaller screens in our homes. New movie repositories have emerged so that with a click of a button we can watch our favorites over and over. Thanks to platforms such as Hulu, Netflix, Amazon Prime, Disney Plus, and HBO Max, we can revisit our favorite movies as often as we want. If that were not enough, we can physically possess the movies we love on DVD or Blu-Ray.

THE SPECIAL FEW

When I was a child, it wasn't possible to own a movie that was formative and impactful in your life. Either you saw it on the big screen of a movie theater or you had to wait until it found its way to television—and so few movies ever made it there. So I did what any child would do. I nudged, pleaded, annoyed, prodded, and begged my parents to take me to see movies in the theater. Lucky for me, I have a brother who is eight years my senior. Why does that matter? My parents would often give him the task of taking his little brother (me!) to the movies when they didn't want to go. Now, that doesn't mean I got to see the movies I wanted to see. But I did get to the movies more than other kids my age. My brother, John, would take me to see movies he wanted to see—movies such as *Jaws* (I couldn't go into the ocean that entire summer after seeing it!) and *Tommy* (all of a sudden I was introduced to the Who and Elton John). Those trips to the theater with my brother had a lasting and positive impact: his movie selections expanded my horizons and opened up a world I otherwise would not have experienced.

Every so often, a movie comes along that you must see. Missing it on the big screen is not an option. The date was May 25, 1977, and it was a Wednesday. An odd day to release a movie! But that was when *Star Wars: A New Hope* was released in theaters. The buzz and anticipation surrounding this movie were enormous.

People stood in long lines to buy tickets to see this movie on a weeknight. And like most children on that day, I wanted—no, I needed!—to go.

I wore my parents down like water eroding the sand on a beach. And they gave in! On Saturday, May 28, 1977, Edward and Louise Skopak did the unimaginable: they took me to the Menlo Park Cinema in Edison, New Jersey. We stood in an outrageously long line for our tickets. We bought a jumbo bucket of popcorn. We sat relatively close to the screen because the theater was full. And then the magic unfurled before our eyes—well, before my eyes at least. I don't think my mother and father were caught up in the *Star Wars* craze. In fact, I'm not sure they stayed awake during the movie! But I was all in. My world changed in those two hours and five minutes. This movie was now a part of me.

At the time, I didn't know the impact *Star Wars* would have on my life. Nor was I aware that this movie would traverse the wild waters of culture and become iconic. This was more than a movie. This movie was now a part of the culture. It would influence language, challenge technological boundaries, and even cause people to think spiritually. *Star Wars* would give birth to ten more films and counting, at the writing of this book.

The *Star Wars* franchise has made more than 10 billion dollars at the box office between its release in 1977 and 2019.[1] This does not include the monies made from comic books, novels, cartoons, toys, video games, costumes, and everything else that comes along with a movie that has become part of the cultural landscape. And now, with Walt Disney Studios owning the franchise, *Star Wars*

1 Ann Schmidt, "Star Wars Day 2020: Here's how much the franchise has made at the box office," *Fox Business*, May 4, 2020, https://www.foxbusiness.com/money/star-wars-day-box-office-profits.

is finding new outlets on the small screen with spin-off shows. But wait! There is even more money to be made: Walt Disney and their global theme parks create rides and attractions—not to mention a high-end resort hotel—so you can be immersed in all things *Star Wars*. All of this is to say that *Star Wars* has found the intersection of cinema and culture, and it is very, very profitable.

THE INTERSECTION OF CINEMA AND CULTURE

Every so often, a movie—like *Star Wars*—becomes interwoven into the fabric of society. It becomes culturally relevant and transformative. The characters, lines, plots, and music transcend the screen and become a part of who we are, what we say, and what we do. What do I mean by culture? Culture is defined by the characteristics and expanding knowledge of a people. The United States Constitution begins, "We the people." Culture is the "we," and the "people" are the many individuals that make up society. Culture encompasses the language (including words and phrases), food, social habits and norms, music, art, sports, entertainment, and just about everything you can think of. Culture is the "we" in which the "people" live. And that culture is expressed, pushed, prodded, challenged, and expanded by what is played out on the big screen.

Maybe the easiest place to see cultural interaction with cinema is in the lines from the movies that are memorized by the audience and shared over and over. The characters and their use of language become a part of our cultural experience. They make us laugh, cry, mourn, celebrate, and search ourselves for deeper expressions of life. You can speak a famous line of a movie without mentioning the movie's name, and people will know the movie it came from and the character who spoke it.

How do I know this? I can't go to a golf course without hearing another golfer quote Carl Spackler, the greenkeeper played by Bill Murray in the movie *Caddyshack*. With a few drops of rain, a golfer will be quick to say, "I don't think the heavy stuff's gonna come down for quite a while." This character and his lines are now a part of the culture. If I mention the words "grave danger," my wife will immediately respond, "Is there another kind?" reminding me that Colonel Nathan Jessup, played by Jack Nicholson in the movie *A Few Good Men*, has added more language to our cultural vocabulary. Movies speak to our hearts and become a frame of reference for our cultural interactions. You can cobble together lines from your favorite movies and carry on a full-blown conversation with another person and be relevant. This is a clear indication that movies are more than entertainment. They are cultural expressions.

THE INTERSECTION OF CULTURE AND FAITH

I am sure that you have been wondering when the topic of faith was going to come up. After all, the book is titled *Christ, Culture, and Cinema*, and the first *C* in this book is *Christ*. As a child of God, you live as an alien in the midst of a cultural storm. Many things in the culture will challenge your good senses, buffet your morality, and wash over your biblically grounded principles. Jesus was aware of the challenges His followers would have living in a cultural hurricane, as His prayer to the Father shows:

> I have given them Your word, and the world has hated them because they are not of the world, just as I am not of the world. I do not ask that You take them out of the world, but that You keep them from the evil one. They are not of the world, just as I am not of the world. (JOHN 17:14–16)

Did you notice what Jesus said? "I do not ask that You take them out of the world." Jesus' desire is that you and I remain in the midst of the culture, the people. Although born anew through the waters of Baptism, claimed by God as His dear child, and blessed with the presence of the Holy Spirit in your life, you are to remain in the midst of the culture. You are to live in the midst of the people and speak faith into the collective "we." You and I have been given the gift of the Holy Scriptures, and we are uniquely equipped to see the spiritual threads that are all around us. The culture sometimes seeks these spiritual threads, but it never really seems to find them. Why? It lacks the lenses of God's Word to see them. Simply put, Jesus is asking us to be the people who speak faith into the collective "we" of our culture.

Being the people who interact and speak faith into the culture may place us in some uncomfortable situations. That is because the culture will drift and move away from Christ-centered faithfulness. One look at the movie industry reveals to us the uphill climb that we have. Since the institution of the movie rating system in 1968, over half of movies released have been rated R.[2] The R rating stands for "restricted," meaning those under age 17 must be accompanied by a parent or adult guardian. In other words, the content may not be appropriate for a young audience—or an

2 Alissa Wilkinson, "Over half of the movies released in the past 50 years were rated R, according to new report," *Vox*, October 30, 2018, https://www.vox.com/culture/2018/10/29/18037982/mpaa-r-rating-report-50-years-criticism.

adult audience! Language, sexually charged content, drug abuse, and violence top the list of why a movie will be tagged with an R rating. And this speaks volumes. If more than 50 percent of the movies made since 1968 have received an R rating, then the culture must be clamoring for them. After all, they are willing to open their wallets and buy the movie tickets and the overpriced buttery popcorn to watch such films.

Where does that leave you and me? Let's take our cue from the apostle Peter:

> You therefore, beloved, knowing this beforehand, take care that you are not carried away with the error of lawless people and lose your own stability. But grow in the grace and knowledge of our Lord and Savior Jesus Christ. To Him be the glory both now and to the day of eternity. Amen. (2 PETER 3:17–18)

When interacting with the culture, you and I need to do a faith check. How are you doing? Where are you in your walk with Jesus? Am I strong enough not to lose the sure footing of my faith?

THE INTERSECTION OF CHRIST, CULTURE, AND CINEMA

And so we arrive at the intersection of the three: Christ, culture, and cinema. What does it look like when these three things meet? At the urging of my son, Jarod, I went with my daughter, Madelyn, to see the movie *Joker*, starring Joaquin Phoenix. *Joker* is rated R. This movie received media criticism, stirred up the law enforcement, frightened theater owners, and created fear regarding the potential violence that might ensue from those embracing chaos and disorder. I have to admit that when I sat down in the darkened theater, I looked around at my fellow moviegoers, trying to discern if they were there to enjoy a movie or cause chaos. What I found was mostly younger people (younger than me, anyway), chomping on chips and popcorn, waiting for the experience of this duly hyped movie—no chaos here.

What unfolded before my eyes was not anything I had expected. The movie was dark, and it kept getting darker right up to the very end. I was not bombarded with violence, bloodshed, and gore (although there was some of that). Rather, I was confronted with a character whose life was molded and shaped by circumstances beyond his control. Arthur Fleck (played by Joaquin Phoenix) is introduced to the audience during a meeting with a social worker, demonstrating profound depression and withdrawal, potentially overmedicated on psychotropic drugs, looking for a glimmer of care, support, and dare I say it, love.

As the movie unfolds, the audience learns that Fleck was adopted by a woman who was mentally unstable. He was abused physically and emotionally as a child by her boyfriend and removed from her home by the state, only to be reunited with her and given the responsibility to care for her as "the man of the house." He lives his life with the false premise planted in his head by his broken mother that he is "happy." Arthur Fleck is anything but happy. The irony is that he is a clown performer who is trying to figure out how to be a stand-up comic. He wants the world to laugh with him, not at him.

But the world laughs, and it laughs hard. Then it turns dark, condescending, reactionary (to his mental and emotional challenges), and in some cases even violent. Pushed to the brink by accomplished and uncompassionate businessmen who physically assault him, Fleck breaks. His emotional and psychological bowl overflows, and chaotic violence ensues: two bodies lay dead in a subway car, with another body dead on a staircase after trying to escape. Gotham City is surprised, shocked, and horrified. The maelstrom that has created the Joker is in abject denial of any complicity in the creation of this chaotic mess.

Welcome to the twenty-first-century intersection of Christ, culture, and cinema. The broken, battered, beaten down, marginalized, and disenfranchised are all around us. Broken families, abused children, and bullying can be found everywhere you look. Social-media feeds are filled with horrible stories, and the societal reaction is almost universally the same: How can this be? How did this happen? We never saw this coming.

Maybe we never saw it coming because we never looked back to see where it was coming from. We failed to see our own failure to help the fractured, broken, and emotionally fragile of our society. We passed the buck and hoped someone farther down the line would help this person that we chose to ignore. But people are valuable! A person's value and worth are found first and foremost in the God of Abraham, Isaac, and Jacob. A person's value is found in the God who "so loved the world, that He sent His only Son" (John 3:16). A person's value is found in the knowledge that God, through Jesus Christ, values you more than anything in the whole universe. This personal value cannot be found in a pill or unearthed by time with a social worker, in the laughter of an audience, or in the overflowing of our emotions as we strike out in unbridled anger. A person's value is found in the One who willingly came and willingly died for you.

Because God willingly did all of this for us, because He came down to us to listen to, touch, heal, and hold broken people, then we, too, should be willing to serve those whom God so highly values. This type of care and compassion means valuing what God values. This type of love and concern means being merciful to those who have not been shown mercy. While Arthur Fleck might be fictional, people like him are all around us: people searching for love and compassion, seeking value and worth, desiring to be understood. They want people to laugh with them and not at them!

I did not want to see *Joker*. I'd much rather go to the movies to drift away in laughter or travel to some made-up science-fiction world. But by going to see this very dark movie, I was reminded of what happens when love doesn't triumph, when mercy doesn't reign, and when compassion is not expressed. As a minister of the Gospel, I was overwhelmed with a sense that I must do more for those worn down by life, the broken, battered, and beaten people who walk silently (and sometimes not so silently) around me in my community. I need to value as Jesus values because every broken life matters to God.

NOW WHAT?

This is what the intersection of Christ, culture, and cinema can do! As we stand at this intersection, Jesus stirs our hearts, enlivens our faith, and pushes us into action. Movies can help us see things in a way that we otherwise wouldn't have seen. Movies show us the culture for what it is and where it stands. Then, armed with our faith in Jesus, we can see where the Word of God needs to go. We see the yearnings of the culture for spiritual direction. We hear the echoes of spiritual truths in a culture that has no biblical direction. That's where we can step up, step in, and serve those around us. At that intersection, we can see and share the story of faith.

So grab your hot, buttered popcorn, pull up a chair, and get ready. The lights are about to go dark. The movie is about to begin. I have chosen a selection of movies with a variety of ratings from G to R. You don't need to watch each movie in its entirety (but you should—you really should!). When I reference a specific scene in a movie, I have included the scene title and the time sequence in the footnotes. If you are not comfortable watching an R-rated movie, that's okay. My descriptions of the various scenes should paint the picture for you, and you're welcome to watch only the specific scene as referenced in the footnote.

Here is your challenge. As you move through the various "scenes" of this book, think about your own intersection with Christ, culture, and cinema. Consider your faith. The Holy Spirit works the gift of faith in us through the Word and Sacraments. We each live out that faith in unique circumstances and specific ways. Next, consider your culture—where you live and what has influenced your life. You bring these things with you when you sit down and watch a movie. My observations in this book have come about because of my intersection of Christ, culture, and cinema. But when you watch the same movies, you may see things that I don't see or experience things I would never have experienced from watching the same movie! That's the fun of cinema. Different people can watch the same movie and yet walk away with different impressions and feelings. You can journey through this book on your own or invite a friend (or a group of friends) to join you. That's up to you. I better stop typing—they just flashed "Please silence your cell phone" on the big screen. The movie is about to begin!

Discussion Questions

Before we venture to the first "scene"—the first chapter and movie discussion—I have some questions for you to consider. Discussion questions are also included after each scene.

1. Where do you like to watch movies—in the theater or at home? Why? What is your favorite genre of movies to watch? Why?

2. What was the first movie you ever saw in a theater? What do you remember about the experience?

3. What is your favorite movie? What movie can you watch over and over?

4. What are your favorite movie lines to quote? What are your favorite Bible verses to quote?

5. What movie triggered thoughts about faith for you? What biblical characters, books of the Bible, or verses of Scripture came to mind because of this movie?

6. Define your culture. What influences have been critical in defining your culture? How has your faith interacted with your culture?

7. What movie has caused you to think spiritually? What movie has caused you to move toward interacting within the culture?

8. What thoughts expressed so far have challenged you?

TICKET
THE END
CINEMA
MOVIE
TICKET
THE END

SCENE 1

ANONYMITY IN THE CROWD

FEATURE PRESENTATION

GLADIATOR

Several years ago, when I lived in the metropolitan New York area, a friend gave me two tickets to see the New York Jets play the Green Bay Packers. It was a cold December afternoon, and everything was on the line. If the Jets won, they were in the playoffs. If the Jets lost, their season was over. The stadium was supercharged that day, enclosing a sea of green-and-white winter coats, hats, gloves, scarves—anything with a New York Jets logo on it to keep you warm. Collectively and collaboratively, the large crowd had become an extension of the team on the field.

In the midst of the delirium and frenzied cheering, a camera zoomed in on one particular fan and projected his image on the large screens around the stadium—a man known to the New York Jets faithful as Fireman Ed. Edwin Anzalone, a New York firefighter during the week and superfan on the weekend, stepped out from the crowd. He was now above the crowd. In a very real way, he was in charge. Perched on top of his brother's shoulders, he brought the 80,242 people packed into the stadium that day to a hushed silence. Then with bravado and fire, he led those same 80,242 people in the famous New York Jets chant: "J-E-T-S! JETS!

JETS! JETS!" The crowd went into a frenzy. The players clearly felt it too! The crowd cheered as one, spoke as one, acted as one.

In that moment, I first came to experience anonymity in the crowd. I was no longer Jeffrey but rather part of something bigger, broader, and beyond myself. And Fireman Ed? He somehow transcended the crowd—above and beyond it, leading, directing, even orchestrating what the crowd would do. At that NFL football game, I experienced a theological moment, a personal conundrum, an uneasy feeling that I was not really in control of myself or my environment. The crowd had swallowed up my individuality, and I felt like I had somehow become anonymous to those around me and even to God Himself! I was no longer in control.

Sometimes, not being in control is okay. The lack of control might be a bit unsettling or bring a sense of loss or fear, but it frees us up to know that we don't have to provide all the answers or solve all the problems. We don't always have to take up the mantle and lead. The real discomfort comes when we realize that anonymity in the crowd is not always healthy or good for us, that within the cover of the crowd, we can get caught up in things that we would never say or do on our own.

WHERE ARE THE CROWDS?

There are so many nooks and crannies of life in which we can find ourselves caught up in the crowd. It's not just in stadiums for sporting events or concerts. In fact, crowds are everywhere:

- a crammed subway or train filled with other commuters
- a shopping mall during the Christmas shopping frenzy

- highways and arteries in and out of the city while driving your car
- church on a Sunday morning
- social media
- a movie theater
- a civil protest
- a political rally

There is hardly a place left in life in which we don't experience a crowd in some form or fashion. But before I go any further, let me explain what I mean by the word *crowd.* A crowd is a large number of people collected together in an identifiable space. With that understanding of crowd, it's not hard to see how we can find ourselves in a crowd, sometimes unintentionally. We may choose to join a crowd. At other times, the crowd is forced upon us. No matter your definition of what makes up a crowd, one thing remains constant: within the confines of the crowd, you can begin to experience a sense of anonymity.

ANONYMITY

When I was standing on my feet, freezing in a football stadium, I experienced a loss of self. My individuality was replaced with the collective of the crowd. We cheered as one, spoke as one, and eventually celebrated as one. The people who surrounded me influenced my feelings, emotions, and thoughts. Think of getting caught in a traffic jam—and I mean a really bad traffic jam. One person blows the horn, then another and another. Next thing you know, a cacophony of automobile horns fills the air with a slightly out-of-tune chorus that expresses to the world, "I have had enough of sitting in this traffic!" Left on your own, you might have been patient and waited for the traffic to subside. But caught up in the measure of the crowd, you joined in with a sense of anonymity as if no one were really holding you accountable for personal expression of anger and impatience.

And yet through the lens of Scripture, we know better. We know that in the eyes of God we are never anonymous. One of those crazy crowd moments happened early in the Book of Genesis, when the mass migration of people settled in the land of Shinar. They had one language in common. Anonymity in the crowd was about to take over:

> They said to one another, "Come, let us make bricks, and burn them thoroughly." And they had brick for stone, and bitumen for mortar. Then they said, "Come, let us build ourselves a city and a tower with its top in the heavens, and let us make a name for ourselves, lest we be dispersed over the face of the whole earth." (GENESIS 11:3–4)

The crowd mentality had taken hold of God's people. All of a sudden, it was no longer about lifting up God. Rather, it was about making their own names great! "Let us make a name for ourselves." No single leader is identified in these verses, and there are no registered complaints from dissenting voices about going forward with any of the plans. The dream, the plan, and the execution all seem to emerge as a group project. And this was some project! A fortified city with walls and a tower in the middle reaching up to the heavens. Collective anonymity in the crowd; nobody is watching; everything will be just fine.

Then the Lord came down to see the city and the tower. Don't miss the irony in that: the tower that was supposed to reach up to the heavens clearly didn't ascend high enough. God had to come down just to see it! And here is the simple truth: the people did not remain anonymous in the crowd. God knew who they were and what they had done. Nobody was excused from their participation in this ill-conceived plan. The consequence? The Lord confused their language and scattered them across the face of the earth. They went from a self-indulgent, celebratory, and industrious crowd to a scattered people drawn out from the anonymity of the grand construction project.

THE CONUNDRUM OF THE CROWD

What happens when the veil of anonymity is removed? What happens when the truth is spoken and the light is shined? In the year 2000, Ridley Scott brought the movie *Gladiator* to the big screen.[3] Set against the backdrop of the Roman Empire circa AD 180, it's a fantastic peek into the impact of the crowd and how easily they are swayed to embrace the wrong as well as the right.

Maximus (played by Russell Crowe) is a powerful and beloved general of the Roman army. He is also loved by the emperor Marcus Aurelius (played by Richard Harris). Marcus summons his family to the battlefront in Germania so that upon victory, he can announce that he will pass the throne over to Maximus instead of to his weaselly son Commodus (played by Joaquin Phoenix). However, Commodus realizes what is about to happen. He murders his father, points the finger at Maximus, and seizes

---

3 *Gladiator*, directed by Ridley Scott (2000; Hollywood, CA: Paramount Pictures, 2017), DVD.

the throne for himself. Maximus is taken into custody. But before Maximus can be executed, he escapes his captors and flees for his home in Spain—only to find his wife and son executed. Broken and defeated, Maximus is picked up along the side of a road by a slave trader and is eventually sold into slavery to Proximo (played by Oliver Reed), a man who trains gladiators. Maximus will live out the remainder of his days as a gladiator.

Maximus's first gladiator encounter is in an old wooden arena somewhere in North Africa. The crowd is filled with bloodlust as they wildly cheer on the combatants. Gladiator battles ended in one of two ways: either one gladiator won, or it was a draw. However, it was the editor who had the final say on whether the loser died or went on to fight again. The editor was the one who oversaw and determined the outcome of gladiatorial battles. Of course, the editor was heavily influenced by—you guessed it—the crowd.

For Maximus, combat was reserved for the battlefield; it was not for sport or entertainment. But on the floor of the gladiator arena, he is forced to use his prowess, skill, and expertise as a Roman soldier, and he makes quick work of six fellow combatants. The encounter ends dramatically as Maximus severs the head off the last combatant (that was gruesome!). The crowd goes from cheering to a hushed silence. In anger and scorn, Maximus throws one of his swords into the editor's booth. The crowd is stirred with fear. Maximus shouts out: "Are you not entertained? Are you not entertained? Is this not why you are here?" He throws down his other sword in disgust and spits on the arena floor. The crowd explodes in wild cheers, chanting, "Spaniard! Spaniard! Spaniard!" The scene fades out with Maximus scanning the crowd. I suspect he's trying to discern why the crowd has exploded in raw emotional support for him. After all, he just brutally murdered six men for the sport and entertainment of the crowd. Maximus knows this is wrong. He is clearly conflicted because of what he has been forced to do. His response? He rebukes the crowd, whose morality has become warped![4]

Our Christian faith paints for us a picture of what is wrong and what is right. Our faith can serve as a moral compass that guides and directs our actions and behaviors. We receive that direction through the Bible as it speaks into our hearts and declares for us what is sinful and what is righteous. Our challenge today is understanding how to apply God's guidance from the Bible to what confronts us in our culture and lives. What do we do when the Word of God doesn't seem so clear or doesn't directly speak to our cultural chaos? We continue to search the Word of God for direction, letting the Holy Spirit speak through the clear passages of Scripture to help us understand how God's Word speaks into our contemporary context.

You probably will never find yourself standing on the floor of a gladiator arena preparing for battle (and thank God for that!), but in today's cultural climate, there's a very good chance you will find yourself standing in a crowd where your faith and values will be challenged and under stress. The world is changing, and it's not necessarily changing for the better. Consider this example: Today, parents host elaborate gender reveals to share with family and friends what is the sex of their yet-to-be-born baby. In contrast to the simplicity of a male or female gender reveal, Facebook kept adding gender options until they finally just created a "custom" option, with which users can define their gender without any restrictions from the platform. So much for the gender reveal!

---

4 To view this scene, watch from 1:06:8 to 1:08:18 (scene 13).

The crowd has declared "what was" is no longer "what is." Things that were previously taken for granted (such as gender identity) are now reshaped, redefined, and reapplied. If you don't like how these things have been culturally changed, then prepare for battle. Chances are that you will find yourself as the outlier voice in the crowd. Make no mistake about it, the crowd is out there waiting to tell you what they think (and in turn, what you are to think as well).

The voice of today's crowd has become loud and vociferous. The crowd declares, "It's our way or the highway!" Civil, peaceable discourse is no longer a part of the crowd vocabulary. This is only heightened and exaggerated where the largest crowds are gathering today: social media. In some respects, social media has become the new gladiator arena. Here, combatants hurl words, insults, and barbs at one another while they are cheered on through reactions of likes, loves, wows, or sad faces! I challenge you to go to your social-media platform of choice and find a socially divisive article. I mean it! Take a moment and do it now. I'll wait. Now scroll through the comments in the article of your choice. Look at how uncivil, unkind, and un-everything people have become with one another. Like Maximus, we stand on the floor of the arena, gazing at the crowd. Maybe you want to throw your proverbial sword into the fray, but to what avail? The crowd has morphed into an angry mob, and there is no room for differing opinions or truth.

Like Maximus, we take in the scene set before us and ponder: Will I be swept away in this chaos? Will my values and, most important, my faith be rent asunder by the tsunami of cultural relevance? How will I remain firm and steadfast in the Word of God when the crowd seemingly wants no part of it?

Standing at this intersection of culture and faith, we realize that this is no small task. It is an intersection fraught with danger and peril. How do we resist the demands of the crowd and remain faithful to our Lord? In the Gospel of Luke, Jesus proclaimed, "Salt is good, but if salt has lost its taste, how shall its saltiness be restored?" (14:34). Jesus says it another way in the Gospel of Matthew: "You are the salt of the earth, but if salt has lost its taste, how shall its saltiness be restored? It is no longer good for anything except to be thrown out and trampled under people's feet" (5:13).

All this talk about salt! I've known some salty people in my life. In fact, I've even been accused of being salty from time to time. But I think Jesus means something very different in these verses. Your faith as a follower of Jesus is without value if it is not genuine. It is nothing but an outward appearance, false bravado, if it is not lived out with authenticity in the midst of the crowd. Let's put it another way: *you* get to spice up the cultural conversation by speaking Law and Gospel into a world that is lawless and faithless. Like Maximus, we have to call it out. We have to challenge the crowd and its way of thinking (and believing). If the crowd balks? So be it. We are being faithful to our Lord and Savior as He has asked us to be. And if the crowd quiets down and listens? Speak, share, and demonstrate truthfulness and faithfulness. Point them to Jesus, and then drop the mic. (Or if you want to be like Maximus, throw the sword!)

THE CROWD GETS WHAT IT WANTS

In today's world, the crowd gets what the crowd wants—just like the crowd in *Gladiator*. If enough people want something, it will be fast-tracked to the marketplace and delivered into the hands of the crowd. Time and time again, ideas are presented, the crowd loves what it sees, and soon everyone seems to have whatever it is. It doesn't matter if it might be hurtful, harmful, or full of side effects. So long as the crowd is happy (and somebody is making a boatload of money off it), so be it!

All of this begs the question: What do people want today? That is the multimillion-dollar question. How can we discern the answer? Here's a little experiment: Take an evening and subject yourself to one hour of news. Choose whatever network you want. It really doesn't matter which one. Just choose one. Next, make sure you have a mix of local, national, and global news stories. Then sit back and let it all pour into your home through your television or smart device. Look at the tapestry of diversity and differing opinions. Gaze upon the brokenness and failings of humankind. See the conflicts, crises, and culture shocks that resound around our communities, nation, and globe. It all leads to a simple conclusion: what the crowd thinks it wants may not be what it needs.

This brings us back to *Gladiator*. In the next pivotal scene, Maximus is about to make his gladiator debut in the Colosseum in Rome. Disguised with helmets and face shields, a group of gladiators are pitted against one another in a group reenactment of the Battle of Zama. In this historic battle, fought in 202 BC, a Roman army led by Scipio defeated the Carthaginian army led by Hannibal. This battle is what the gladiators are to reenact before the large crowd in the Colosseum. And Maximus and his band are cast in the role of Hannibal and the Carthaginian army, doomed to failure. It's what the people want, and it's what is supposed to be delivered to the crowd.

Except Maximus has a different idea. What the crowd wants isn't necessarily what the crowd will get. As Maximus and his men stand on the Colosseum floor, waiting for whatever will come out from behind the doors, he asks his fellow gladiators if any have military experience. Why? Because whatever comes out of the gates will demand precision and teamwork for survival. At that moment, the gates open wide and chariots with armed warriors descend upon Maximus and his fellow gladiators, who are all on foot. It's what the crowd wants! It what's the crowd demands!

However, Maximus will not stand for this staged tragedy. He coordinates his men and turns the battle on its ear. Chariots are knocked over and combatants are scattered, all while Maximus, sitting on a white horse taken from a defeated enemy, wielding a sword and barking out orders, remains defiant to the will of the crowd.[5] The crowd is confused, as is Commodus, the Roman Emperor and villain of the movie. They didn't get what they wanted.

It's not unlike the disappointed look of a child on Christmas morning when he or she rips into a smartly wrapped Christmas present, only to find a new pair of socks! "It's not what I wanted," the child exclaims. But it might be exactly what the child needed. And that is where society is today. Everything promises to be the best and brightest, but once the wrapping paper is torn away, we are left with disappointment. Our expectations and anticipations have not been met, and we are left looking for the next cultural promise to fill the void.

Even as followers of Jesus, we can get caught up in the expectations and anticipations of the world. We can project our hopes, wants, and desires on God. But that doesn't mean God will

5 To view this scene, watch from 1:21:25 to 1:28:59 (scene 15).

acquiesce to our plans. In fact, we are like the crowd; sometimes what we need isn't what we want or what we have hoped for—it's really about God. The Bible instructs us that He alone can and will address our needs and carry our burdens. And He will do it according to His plan, in His way, and in His time.

My favorite postresurrection story really expresses the intersection of culture and faith when it comes to our wants versus our deepest needs. On the day of the resurrection, two of Jesus' followers were heading back home to Emmaus (a seven-mile trip). These two people were disappointed, broken, and filled with sorrow. As they were walking and talking about all of the things they had witnessed regarding Jesus—and I'm pretty confident they were talking about His arrest, trial, beating, and death on the cross—lo and behold, Jesus sidles up next to them. But here's the twist: they were prevented from recognizing Jesus. Here's what happened next.

> And He [Jesus] said to them, "What is this conversation that you are holding with each other as you walk?" And they stood still, looking sad. Then one of them, named Cleopas, answered Him, "Are You the only visitor to Jerusalem who does not know the things that have happened there in these days?" And He said to them, "What things?" And they said to Him, "Concerning Jesus of Nazareth, a man who was a prophet mighty in deed and word before God and all the people, and how our chief priests and rulers delivered Him up to be condemned to death, and crucified Him. But we had hoped that He was the one to redeem Israel. Yes, and besides all this, it is now the third day since these things happened. Moreover, some women of our company amazed

> us. They were at the tomb early in the morning, and when they did not find His body, they came back saying that they had even seen a vision of angels, who said that He was alive. Some of those who were with us went to the tomb and found it just as the women had said, but Him they did not see." And He said to them, "O foolish ones, and slow of heart to believe all that the prophets have spoken! Was it not necessary that the Christ should suffer these things and enter into His glory?" And beginning with Moses and all the Prophets, He interpreted to them in all the Scriptures the things concerning Himself. (LUKE 24:17–27)

After recounting all of the agonizing details of what happened to Jesus (and I'm not really sure how Jesus kept a straight face in this exchange!), Cleopas expresses the most agonizing and heartfelt words: "But we had hoped that He was the one to redeem Israel" (v. 21). Hope unfulfilled. Hope dashed on the rocks of life. Hope buried in a tomb in a garden. Hope. These two disciples had to face the idea that Jesus was not the Messiah they had hoped He would be. Their expectations and anticipations did not match the reality of a cross and a tomb. They didn't get what they wanted!

But in the midst of their despair and disappointment—in not receiving the Messiah they envisioned or dreamed of—Jesus had compassion on them in their foolishness. Jesus takes the time to walk the disciples through the Scriptures to reveal to them the truth. He loves them as they have never been loved and gives them a hope beyond anything they could have ever imagined.

So what is it that you want? Are you like the crowds, clamoring for the next and greatest thing? Or are you searching for something different? something fulfilling? something the world simply cannot provide? Maybe we need to take our cue from the crowd in the Colosseum who have just witnessed Maximus rewrite history. Maybe we need to look through unfiltered eyes and see what God really wants us to see. Maybe what we want isn't what we need, and that's okay because what we really need—love, mercy, grace, and forgiveness—God is providing in abundance through His Son, Jesus.

THE CROWD HAS POWER

It's an incredible experience when you are caught up in the emotional yo-yo of a crowd, from wild cheering to hushed groans, angry shouts to cries of adoration. When the crowd is caught off guard and thoroughly surprised, the reaction is priceless. Maybe this is why people love going to sporting events, concerts, plays, and movies. We enter an emotional space together in which we share the journey with one another. My feelings are validated by the feelings of those around me. My reactions are affirmed by the reactions of those who are sharing in this moment with me.

Let's consider how this plays out in the movie *Gladiator*. Maximus and his fellow gladiators (acting out the roles of the Carthaginian army led by Hannibal) have just rewritten history by defeating the competing gladiators, who were portraying the Roman army led by Scipio. The crowd is brought to their feet. They are wildly cheering and exalting this amazing turn of events on the Colosseum floor. As the crowds continue their collective celebration, the Roman emperor, the coward Commodus, enters the arena floor to meet the hero of the gladiatorial moment.

As Maximus rises to his feet, the crowd stills so they can hear the exchange between Commodus and the hero. Commodus wants to know who this mysterious gladiator is. The tension is almost unbearable! Maximus refuses to reveal his identity, refers to himself by the generic term *gladiator*, then turns his back and walks away from the emperor. An insult beyond forgiveness! The emperor is incensed! He demands to be honored by this gladiator!

The crowd is stunned! The gasps can be heard around the Colosseum. Slowly and deliberately, Maximus turns to face the emperor, the man who tried to have him killed and who murdered his family. He removes his helmet and face shield to reveal his identity: the beloved general and friend of Commodus's father; the great leader of the Roman army; the husband and father to a slain wife and son; and a man who will gain his vengeance! One thing is for sure: the crowd in the Colosseum didn't see that coming; nor did Commodus!

When Commodus makes the move to have his guards execute Maximus, the crowd takes over, chanting, "Live!" over and over. In a climactic moment, though wanting to be rid of his foe, the emperor succumbs to the demand of the crowd and gives the thumbs-up for Maximus to live. The Colosseum erupts with frantic and frenzied cheers.[6] The crowd has influenced the decision and won the moment. Maximus stands in awe of the power of the crowd. To the cheers and accolades, he lifts his helmet in the air. It is to the crowd that he owes his life.

A large crowd united in thought can strike fear in a person whose motives or actions are contrary to the crowd. Just look at Commodus in this scene. He wants Maximus dead and gone. But the crowd has other ideas. The crowd has fallen in love with their gladiator, and no harm should befall him. And who in their

---

6 To view this scene, watch from 1:28:59 to 1:32:55 (scene 16).

right mind would cross a stadium full of people who are united in thought and potentially in deed?

In our intersection of faith and culture, it is not hard for the Christian to understand the power and impact of such a crowd. After all, the story of our salvation was framed by crowds. In a week's time, the crowds exerted great pressure on those in leadership—first to fear Jesus and later to have Him executed.

Take a look at what happens when the time is right and Jesus enters Jerusalem:

> The next day the large crowd that had come to the feast heard that Jesus was coming to Jerusalem. So they took branches of palm trees and went out to meet Him, crying out, "Hosanna! Blessed is He who comes in the name of the Lord, even the King of Israel!" (JOHN 12:12–13)

This is big! This is really big! This crowd is pushing their agenda, crying "Hosanna," which means, "Save us now! Save us, we pray!" Save them from what? From the foreign subjugation that was their lot under the Roman Empire. The crowd clearly expects Jesus to answer and solve their earthly problems immediately. He who healed the sick, restored sight to the blind, made the lame to walk, and raised the dead—certainly, He could take care of those pesky Romans and make life all better. That is what the crowd seems to think.

And what about the Pharisees? As religious leaders, they are not comfortable with what is unfolding before their eyes. "So the Pharisees said to one another, 'You see that you are gaining nothing. Look, the world has gone after Him'" (v. 19). They are keenly aware that such a crowd is not easily opposed or scattered. They understand that such a crowd (and especially the one they are exalting, namely, Jesus) threatens their authority and leadership. I suspect if the Pharisees were to watch *Gladiator*, they could relate to Commodus on the arena floor—to do what you really want to do might cause your own demise.

And yet to this day, we remember this crowd with their palm branches, cloaks on the road, and shouts of "Hosanna in the highest!" (Mark 11:10). In fact, we join in with this crowd every year when Holy Week rolls around. We wave palm branches, we sing "Hosanna, Loud Hosanna," and we rejoice that the King has come. But—and there always seems to be a *but* in these jubilant moments—the crowd will turn in less than a week. Crowds can be fickle. In fact, crowds can turn 180 degrees when we least expect it. One moment they are cheering, and the next moment they are hurling insults and murderous threats.

The next time we meet the crowd during Holy Week, Jesus is standing before Pilate, set against Barabbas, a notorious criminal. Look at how it all unfolds:

> When they [the crowds] had gathered, Pilate said to them, "Whom do you want me to release for you: Barabbas, or Jesus who is called Christ?" For he knew that it was out of envy that they [the Sadducees] had delivered Him up. Besides, while he was sitting on the judgment seat, his wife sent word to him, "Have nothing to do with that righteous man, for I have suffered much because of Him today in a dream." Now the chief priests and the elders persuaded the crowd to ask for Barabbas and destroy Jesus. The governor again said to them, "Which of the two do you want me to release for you?" And they said, "Barabbas." Pilate said to them, "Then what shall I do with Jesus who is called

> Christ?" They all said, "Let Him be crucified!" And he said, "Why? What evil has He done?" But they shouted all the more, "Let Him be crucified!" (MATTHEW 27:17–23)

Just like that—with a little nudging from the chief priests and elders—the crowd goes from shouting, "Hosanna!" to shouting, "Let Him be crucified!" And in the midst of it all stands Jesus, knowing that His divine mission lies ahead on a cross, where the crowd's call for crucifixion will deliver the forgiveness of sins the world so desperately needs.

It may be that many of the people who cried "Hosanna" and shouted "Crucify" were also there at the cross. I would imagine that some of those same people hurled those painful insults, "You who would destroy the temple and rebuild it in three days, save Yourself! If You are the Son of God, come down from the cross" (Matthew 27:40). But isn't that the nature of a crowd? Within the confines of a crowd, people begin to feel anonymous. The group takes over, and the individual is left behind. These are no longer my words but the words of something larger, bigger, and beyond me. These are the words of the crowd. The words express the collective thoughts and feelings of the crowd; they are not simply my intellectual property. These words belong to the crowd. And so leaders tremble, names separate from faces, the crowd cries out, and the individual fades into perceived anonymity.

BUT I'M NOT ANONYMOUS

However, as our faith, culture, and cinema intersect, we realize there really isn't anonymity in the crowd. In fact, our words, actions, attitudes, and behaviors are on display for the world to see. Today, video cameras are everywhere. Simply walk into any movie theater, shopping mall, arena, or stadium, and look around. There are cameras everywhere, watching and recording your every move. Even when the space is really crowded, don't think for one moment that you are covered by group anonymity.

But more important, it's not just security and law enforcement watching over your shoulder. The Bible tells us that the Lord knows His own and calls you by name (see Isaiah 43:1). No matter how crowded the world may become, you are still known to our creating, loving, and redeeming God. Jesus tells us that "even the hairs of your head are all numbered" (Luke 12:7), and He says, "I am the good shepherd. I know My own and My own know Me" (John 10:14). There is a profound comfort in these words. No matter how crowded the world becomes, no matter how fickle the crowd can be, no matter how swept up in the moment you find yourself, Jesus knows you, loves you, forgives you, and redeems you.

The movie *Gladiator*, although focusing on the tension between Maximus and Commodus, gives keen insight into the cultural phenomena of crowds and crowd behavior. With sweeping cinematic bravado, we hear, feel, and experience the overwhelming power and emotions of the crowd. We are reminded that we, too, can get caught up in the crowd—whether it be in traffic, shopping malls, arenas, stadiums, or even our social-media feed. The world is a crowded place and getting more crowded every day. But despite the sense of anonymity that can come over us in the crowd, we know that we are not anonymous. We are known to God.

Discussion Questions

1. Identify a time when you were part of a crowd. How did it make you feel? Did you get caught up in the moment? Why or why not?

2. List places in your community where you find and experience crowds today.

3. When have you experienced anonymity in the crowd? What actions, words, or behaviors did you engage in? How did it make you feel?

4. Read Genesis 11:1–9. What has the crowd done wrong? Why does God respond the way He does?

5. In *Gladiator*, Maximus calls out the crowd for their behavior. Why is it hard for you to speak out in our cultural climate today? How can we speak Law and Gospel into our communities?

6. How does society react today when it does not get what it wants? How does our faith speak to the needs of our society? Why is Jesus what we need? How does He demonstrate that in Luke 24:13–35?

7. In *Gladiator*, the crowd had the power to influence Commodus to spare Maximus's life. In the crowds that surrounded Jesus during Holy Week, who had the power? Who was in control?

8. What challenged you in this scene? What did you find affirming to your faith?

TICKET
THE END
CINEMA
MOVIE
TICKET
THE END

SCENE 2

FOLLOW THE LEADER

FEATURE PRESENTATION

TOY STORY

The English language is filled with words that are spelled the same way but have drastically different meanings depending on how they are applied in a sentence. These are known as *homographs.* For example, *bass* can be a fish or a low, deep voice. *Minute* can be a measure of time or mean small in size or stature. *Bat* can be a piece of sports equipment or a winged animal.

The word *lead* is another homograph. On one hand, *lead* is a chemical element (Pb) and is assigned the atomic number 82 on the periodic table of elements. It is a heavy metal that is soft, malleable, and toxic. On the other hand, *lead* can be used as a verb to describe the actions of a person in charge of others—moving people toward a specific direction or preferred future. The person who leads typically engenders trust and confidence in those who follow.

And yet, these two meanings intertwine when we consider the words *leader* and *leadership*, especially in the life and breadth of the Church. A poor leader can bring a ministry team down. Leaders can become like a boat anchor that holds a church or ministry in place as they sink to the bottom, dragging everyone along with them. This kind of leader is viewed as "soft"—typically possessing weak guiding principles and no sense of direction or plan. Because these leaders lack a plan, they are constantly changing direction according to the suggestions and whims of those in their charge, thus rendering them malleable. This kind of leader is ultimately toxic, causing the church or community to flounder and eventually fail. In a very real way, the leader has become lead—an embodiment of the atomic number 82 on the periodic table of elements.

Standing in stark contrast to the lead leader is the leader who leads. This kind of leader builds people up, making tasks lighter and easier for those who follow. Such leaders remain firm to their beliefs and values while casting a vision for the future. These leaders have a clear plan and adjust the plan accordingly as they encounter bumps and hiccups along the way. However, they focus on the goals that are set before those in their care and charge. This kind of leader is ultimately energizing and beloved, lifting up the community and filling it with a spirit of unity. This kind of leader embodies leadership—translating vision into reality.

LEADERS WANTED, INQUIRE WITHIN

Whether they are lead leaders or leaders who lead, people occupying the role of leader are all around us: in schools, businesses, social organizations, government, sports teams, and volunteer organizations, just to name a few. Wherever people gather and organize, the need for leaders becomes apparent, and people find their way to these roles (whether they are capable or not).

Leaders come to their positions in a number of ways: elected, appointed, hired, and even as a volunteer. More often than not, they set about demonstrating their abilities to make their leadership capability known to others. In some cases, they have to campaign or advertise their abilities to make themselves known to those whom they desire to lead. Others step out from the midst of the people and provide leadership where there is a void. When enough people get behind the individual—voilà! A leader is identified, elected, hired, or placed in the position.

But sometimes people are swept into leadership roles because nobody else is willing to do so. Institutional lethargy, unraveling organizational structures, inadequate funding, and fractured unity cause leaders to flee, leaving a leadership void whereby the mentality of "I must do this because no one else will" creeps into the door. The leaders have fled, and the ill-equipped are now trying to stave off the unraveling of the organization. The person who is caught stepping into this failing organization ends up expending vast amounts of emotional and physical energy simply trying to prevent institutional death.

Thus, the need remains the same: whether in a business or a club, a government or a church, there is a profound need for leaders. The very best leaders are known to those even beyond the ones they serve. These people become closely identifiable to the mission and purpose of whatever the organization may be. You don't think of one without the other; they are like peanut butter and jelly. For example, mention the name Bill Gates and what comes to mind? Microsoft. Derek Jeter? The New York Yankees. Martin Luther King Jr.? The civil rights movement. Margaret Thatcher? The first woman prime minister of Great Britain.

LEADERS IN THE CHURCH

If you grew up in the church, think back to the church of your childhood. You probably remember the services and potlucks, the sanctuary and the singing. But if you really think about it, you remember the various people who were leaders in your church. Sunday School teachers, elders, church council members, the people who took care of the property and grounds, altar guild members, and ushers—these people were leaders in your church. They gave freely and willingly for the care and advancement of the ministry. They used their gifts and talents for the sake of the church and for the care and well-being of the members. And with whom did these leaders work closely? The pastor, the leader who was up in the front of the church. If you think back to the church of your childhood, you more than likely remember the pastor—his voice, presence, and position in the life of your church.

The reason you remember the pastor is because a pastor is a lot of things: preacher, teacher, Bible scholar, homebound-visitor, pray-er, baptizer, wedding planner, just to name a few. In the life of the church, the pastor seems to be everywhere all the time. In fact, when he's not there, the people tend to be concerned! "Where's the pastor?" "Is he okay?" "Maybe we should call him and make sure!" It's as if the people are fearful to take a step, have an activity, or simply gather without their pastor.

The reason for this institutional concern can be summarized in one little word: *leader*. The pastor is the leader of the people who have rightly called him to serve in this divinely appointed office. The Lutheran Church teaches that "no one should publicly teach in the Church, or administer the Sacraments, without a rightly ordered call."[7] Call it what you will—sacramental leadership, biblical leadership, Christian leadership, pastoral leadership—this *rite vocatus* means that the bearer of the office has the proper public authority to exercise leadership from the office he now occupies. And that leadership is over the congregation that has called him to be their pastor—no more and no less.

What does this leader in the Church do? The tip-off to the answer is found in how the Church addresses this leader: *pastor*. The word *pastor* finds its origin in Latin and means "shepherd" or "herdsman." However, last I checked, pastors weren't taking their congregations out to fields so that they could graze! Rather, a pastor follows the metaphorical example as presented in the Old and New Testaments. Both Testaments consistently use the word *shepherd* to describe the one who watches over the flock of God's people.

Psalm 23, also referred to as the shepherd's psalm, is probably the best-known psalm. In the opening words, the psalmist states, "The LORD is my shepherd" (v. 1). This tells us plainly who is the only perfect shepherd: the Lord. According to Psalm 23, it is the Lord who richly and abundantly provides for our physical, spiritual, and emotional needs on a daily basis. In fact, a quick scan of the psalm shows us how much the Lord does for the sake of the sheep, namely, you and me:

- "He makes me lie down in green pastures" (v. 2a).
- "He leads me beside still waters" (v. 2b).
- "He leads me in paths of righteousness" (v. 3).

---

7 AC XIV; *Concordia: The Book of Concord*, second edition (St. Louis: Concordia Publishing House, 2006), 39.

- "You are with me; Your rod and Your staff, they comfort me" (v. 4).
- "You prepare a table before me in the presence of my enemies" (v. 5a).
- "You anoint my head with oil" (v. 5b).

The Lord's care for His people is abundant and full. The Lord pours out His blessings on His people over and over and over again. And this care doesn't stop at the grave, as the psalm makes clear: "I shall dwell in the house of the LORD forever" (v. 6).

Okay, so the Lord is *the* Shepherd. Scripture makes that abundantly clear. In fact, in the New Testament, Jesus states, "I am the good shepherd. The good shepherd lays down His life for the sheep" (John 10:11). Connecting the theological dots is not very difficult: The Lord is the Shepherd. Jesus, God in flesh, is the Shepherd who willingly died on the cross for you and me, His sheep. Where then does this leave the Church and those who occupy the rightly called office of pastor?

OTHER SHEPHERDS?

The Good Shepherd, Jesus, never intended for His people to wander as sheep without a physical shepherd in their presence. The Gospel of Matthew gives us a very clear picture of the Good Shepherd's heart:

> And Jesus went through all the cities and villages, teaching in their synagogues and proclaiming the gospel of the kingdom and healing every disease and every affliction. When He saw the crowds He had compassion for them, because

> they were harassed and helpless, like sheep without a shepherd. Then He said to His disciples, "The harvest is plentiful, but the laborers are few; therefore pray earnestly to the Lord of the harvest to send out laborers into the harvest." (MATTHEW 9:35–38)

Sheep are not meant to be scattered; rather, they are to be gathered. And who gathers the sheep? Shepherds, of course!

In 1995, director John Lasseter and Pixar Animation Studios created a wholly computer-animated movie, the first of its kind: *Toy Story*. Released by Walt Disney Pictures, the film features the voices of Tom Hanks as Woody the cowboy and Tim Allen as Buzz Lightyear, a space ranger superhero. And yes, both characters are toys. Along with other toys (which include Mr. Potato Head, Slinky Dog, Bo Peep and her sheep, Etch-a-Sketch, Viewfinder, Rex the dinosaur, little green army men, and a remote-controlled car, to name a few), they make up the "sheep" of their owner, Andy. Andy, a young boy, loves his toys and marks them as his own by writing his name on them.[8]

But Andy is not the shepherd. No, the role of leadership amongst the toys goes to Woody. Woody has a special role in the life of Andy's room. He is clearly the shepherd, the leader, of the toys. But there is great anxiety amongst the toys in Andy's room. The family is moving, and Andy is going to have a birthday party prior to the move—and that means new toys, toys that could either complement or replace them! Tension and fear about their unknown future unfold downstairs at the birthday party![9] Presents,

8 *Toy Story*, directed by John Lasseter (1995; Burbank, CA: Buena Vista Home Entertainment, 2019), DVD.

9 To view these scenes, watch from 6:35 to 19:18 (scene 4, "The Staff Meeting") and 9:19 to 14:16 (scene 5, "Recon Plan Charlie").

boxes, endless possibilities. Woody does what leaders do: he takes charge of the situation while trying to assuage the fears of those he serves. Even though he has his own fears, he suppresses those feelings for the sake and care of those he leads.

No human leader is perfect—far from it! And nor is our animated friend Woody. He has a sense of arrogance, of knowing more than those he serves. When trouble arises, he is quick to jump into the fray and push aside the other toys to get the job done. Although Woody is still in charge, he shows the flaws and fissures of imperfect leadership when a crisis arises.

When leaders believe they are in control of a situation, they exhibit a sense of invincibility. Nothing could possibly go wrong. Take, for example, the apostle Peter. When Jesus summoned a "staff meeting" with His disciples—the future leaders of the Early Christian Church—He asked them a simple question: "Who do people say that the Son of Man is?" (Matthew 16:13). It's really not that difficult a question, is it? After all, the disciples had witnessed miracles, heard His teaching with authority, and been in His presence consistently for months on end. This should not be that hard!

And for Peter, it's not. His answer was bold, declarative: "You are the Christ, the Son of the living God" (Matthew 16:16). Because of Peter's bold and confident proclamation, Jesus praised Peter and showered him with accolades and promises for the future Church and his leadership.

If only the story ended there! When Jesus pressed Peter and the other disciples regarding His arrest, beating, death, and resurrection, Peter was emboldened. He took Jesus aside and rebuked Him. Let me say that again: *Peter rebuked Jesus.* This was not a good move. Remember, Jesus is *the* Good Shepherd. Peter, on the other hand, is an undershepherd of the Good Shepherd. The result? A rebuke from Jesus: "Get behind Me, Satan! You are a hindrance to Me. For you are not setting your mind on the things of God, but on the things of man" (Matthew 16:23).

The leaders of the Church are not all that different from Peter and Woody. There are moments when they are spot-on. They confidently lead the people of God and care for the flock in extraordinary ways. They proclaim Christ and are quick to bring comfort and peace, even when people are restless and fearful.

Consider how your pastor brought you comfort in the past. Maybe you are old enough to remember the terrorist attacks of September 11, 2001, and how your pastor faithfully cared for and led your church through the storm. Maybe your time stamp is the economic crash of 2008, when finding any job or meaningful work was nearly impossible. And yet, there was your pastor, ever vigilant, leading your church and caring for your soul. Or maybe you are simply thinking of recent events: March 2020, when the wild uncertainty of COVID-19 became a household word, closing the doors to public gatherings for weeks and months on end. But there was your pastor, leading online worship services, Bible studies, and devotions to keep you connected to the remainder of the flock.

Now, stop and consider that these undershepherds are not *the* Good Shepherd. They, too, have fears and frailties, anxieties and anxiousness, worries and weaknesses. Like Woody, they may lose their cool, pushing others out of the way just to get the task done. They may become like Peter, rebuking Jesus because he didn't want harm to befall Him. So, too, the pastor is wobbled and wearied by the tumult of the times.

Typically, I am a pastor who is in control of my emotions (oh, that's right; I'm a pastor, if you didn't figure that out already). But toward the end of the COVID-19 quarantine in 2020, I was emotionally and intellectually worn out. Leading worship online from our gymnasium because we were in the midst of a sanctuary renovation project, trying to keep my teachers and school positive while having to switch to online education, and making sure all the bases of ministry were covered, I had become an overly emotional leader—so much so that my principal and associate pastor were genuinely worried about my well-being. They approached my council and elders with their concerns. In turn, the church gave me a monthlong sabbatical to recover, recharge, and reenergize for the ministry year ahead of us. I was like Woody, pushing people out of the way to put the batteries in the right way. I was like Peter, rebuking Jesus so that no harm or ill would befall Him. To put it bluntly, I was one tired shepherd. My leadership emotions had run amuck. And that's okay, because, after all, I am an undershepherd of the Good Shepherd—and only He is perfect!

LEADERS STUMBLE, TUMBLE, AND ARE RESTORED

However, being tired isn't the only reason shepherds find themselves in trouble. We need to remember that the pastor-shepherd-leader is a human being—a fallen, sinful human being. They don't always get it right. In fact, there are many times when emotions like pride, greed, jealousy, and anger cloud their vision. One of the most relatable and emotional moments in the movie *Toy Story* paints a picture of a leader not getting it right. Andy and his friends have just burst into his room and dropped Buzz Lightyear on the bed, and in so doing, they pushed Woody off the bed and onto the floor.

Buzz Lightyear is flashy and exciting. He has flashing lights, buttons, an electronic voice, and retractable wings. Woody, on the other hand, has a simple pull string on his back to make him talk. Woody tries to defend his territory against the newcomer and exert his right to lead.[10] But times are changing, and there is another leader in the midst of Andy's toys—and an intergalactic space ranger at that!

Leaders don't always get it right, and sometimes they get it horribly wrong. This will be displayed in their words, attitudes, actions, and behaviors. Removed from his rightful place of leadership (Andy's bed) and relegated to the toy box, Woody reaches his breaking point.[11] In a moment of haste and anger, Woody triggers a series of events that causes Buzz Lightyear to plummet from the second-story window of Andy's room into the danger and unknown of the world outside. In a defining moment, Woody becomes a fallen leader.

Unfortunately, this is nothing new. Take Jesus' disciple Peter. Although bold in his proclamation that Jesus is "the Christ, the Son of the Living God" (Matthew 16:16), when pressed on the eve of Jesus' crucifixion, Peter sang a very different tune. Preservation of position and self can be a powerful elixir. Look what Peter did, not once but three times, when asked if he knew Jesus:

- The servant girl at the door said to Peter, "You also are not one of this man's disciples, are you?" He said, "I am not." (JOHN 18:17)

---

10 To view this scene, watch from 14:17 to 20:09 (scene 6, "Buzz Lightyear Space Ranger").

11 To view these scenes, watch from 22:17 to 24:24 (scene 8, "Woody and Buzz") and 26:01 to 29:27 (scene 10, "Who Will Andy Pick?").

- Now Simon Peter was standing and warming himself. So they said to him, "You also are not one of His disciples, are you?" He denied it and said, "I am not." (JOHN 18:25)
- One of the servants of the high priest, a relative of the man whose ear Peter had cut off, asked, "Did I not see you in the garden with Him?" Peter again denied it. (JOHN 18:26–27)

Peter's desire for self-preservation superseded his faithful walk with Jesus. Sin clouded his judgment, and selfishness ruled the day. And don't think for one moment this doesn't apply to the conversation of Church and leadership. It is like the long-tenured pastor who, after his retirement, doggishly hinders the church from embracing their new pastor; it is the church council member who refuses to allow a new member to step into a position of leadership; it is the traditionalists who crush any attempt at new ideas or ministries from happening in "their church." As a result, feelings are hurt, people are pushed aside (or out the window like Buzz Lightyear), and ministry is stifled or snuffed out.

Like all humans, leaders stumble and tumble because of their sinful nature. But we have a Lord and Savior who loves us and restores us as His dear children. In one of the most moving turns of Jesus' postresurrection ministry, He takes the time to love and restore Peter:

> When they had finished breakfast, Jesus said to Simon Peter, "Simon, son of John, do you love Me more than these?" He said to Him, "Yes, Lord; You know that I love You." He said to him, "Feed My lambs." He said to him a second time, "Simon, son of John, do you love Me?" He said to Him, "Yes, Lord; You know that I love You." He said to him, "Tend My sheep." He said to him the third time, "Simon, son of John,

> do you love Me?" Peter was grieved because He said to him the third time, "Do you love Me?" and he said to Him, "Lord, You know everything; You know that I love You." Jesus said to him, "Feed My sheep." (JOHN 21:15–17)

The restoration of Peter to his position of leadership is grounded in reconciliation and affirmed in love. And Peter is not merely forgiven! He is also pressed back into his role of leadership for the sake of the Church! Consider what Jesus directs Peter to do: feed and tend to the sheep. That is the Church. Is Peter a leader who stumbles and tumbles? Absolutely! But he is also a leader who is loved by His Savior and restored to do even greater things than these!

The good news is that this same Jesus loves and restores us through a heartfelt call to repentance, confession, and forgiveness. The same Jesus who asked Peter, "Do you love Me?" asks us the same question. This is so critical to the life of the Church. When the disciples asked Jesus how they were to pray, it was no accident that Jesus included the words, "Forgive us our sins as we forgive those who sin against us." Martin Luther explains this phrase in the Small Catechism:

> We pray in this petition that our Father in heaven would not look at our sins, or deny our prayer because of them. We are neither worthy of the things for which we pray, nor have we deserved them, but we ask that He would give them all to us by grace, for we daily sin much and surely deserve nothing but punishment. So we too will sincerely forgive and gladly do good to those who sin against us.[12]

12 Small Catechism, Fifth Petition; *Luther's Small Catechism with Explanation* (St. Louis: Concordia Publishing House, 2017), 21.

Stumbling, tumbling, and restored. No leader inside (or outside) of the Church is perfect, no matter if that person is called, ordained, elected, or volunteering. But through a life of confession and forgiveness in Christ, each is forgiven and restored.

EVERY SHEEP MATTERS TO THE SHEPHERD

Just as the undershepherds matter to the Good Shepherd, Jesus, so, too, does every sheep matter to the undershepherds. Leaders may lose energy and get run down, stumble, and tumble, but even greater is the pain when a leader loses even one sheep. In the movie *Toy Story*, when Woody and Buzz Lightyear find themselves trying to reconnect with Andy at Pizza Planet, Woody takes on the mantle of leadership. He has a plan, he knows the way, and he's ready to execute! There is just one small problem: Buzz Lightyear has a different plan in mind. Like a wandering sheep, Buzz has strayed to a rocket-ship-themed crane game, hoping the "rocket" can take them to Andy. But rather than saving them, Buzz has jumped into the middle of imminent danger.[13]

When Woody sees what has happened to Buzz, he steps up. Woody willingly puts himself in harm's way to rescue Buzz, abandoning their chance to reunite with Andy. Woody crawls into the crane game and grabs at Buzz, who has been snared by the claw of the game (controlled by the sadistic Sid, the enemy of all toys). The toy aliens with them in the game try to stop Woody, saying that Buzz "has been chosen." But Woody clings to Buzz while fending off the rubber aliens and decrying, "Stop it! Stop it, you zealots!"

---

13 To view this scene, watch from 35:09 to 39:24 (scene 13, "Pizza Planet").

Woody is demonstrating the kind of shepherd leadership Jesus talks about in the Gospel of Luke. Tax collectors and sinners were attracted to Jesus' ministry. These were not socially acceptable folk, especially in religious society. In fact, these were the people who lived on the fringes, in the shadows, on the outside looking in. And yet, these are the very people Jesus visits, listens to, dines with, and heals. These are the lost who need to be found and welcomed in. Look at the parable Jesus tells about the lost and found:

> What man of you, having a hundred sheep, if he has lost one of them, does not leave the ninety-nine in the open country, and go after the one that is lost, until he finds it? And when he has found it, he lays it on his shoulders, rejoicing. And when he comes home, he calls together his friends and his neighbors, saying to them, "Rejoice with me, for I have found my sheep that was lost." Just so, I tell you, there will be more joy in heaven over one sinner who repents than over ninety-nine righteous persons who need no repentance. (LUKE 15:3–7)

And if that weren't enough, Jesus goes on to reinforce this understanding of seeking and saving the lost with two more parables (the lost coin in Luke 15:8–10 and the prodigal son in Luke 15:11–32). The point of all of this is simple: the leader willingly goes out, seeks the lost, and celebrates upon finding and restoring the lost!

The difficult question for the Church to ask today is this: Do we really desire to seek the lost? Society has become a muddled and messy place. Our values and sense of right have been stretched, pulled, and challenged at every turn. What we have always known as right is now considered prudish, outdated, and wrong. As people drift further away from a biblical understanding of right and wrong, how eager are we to walk out into the darkened landscape to seek and save the lost? How eager are we to dive into the rocket-ship crane game?

But maybe there is an even more challenging thought for the Church today: what happens when the broken, fractured, sinful world hears the Gospel, receives it, and joyfully comes through the doors? As the pastor-shepherd-leader embraces the broken sinner who has now entered our midst, do we find ourselves more like the rubber aliens in the crane game, pushing the pastor aside as they did Woody so that the sinner would leave our midst?

The tapestry of ministry is made of a wide variety of sheep, many of whom are righteous and faithful people. But there are many who are not! For many, the past is messy and macabre, and their lives are littered with brokenness, hurt, violence, and self-inflicted wounds. They are filled with despair and depression. And the shepherd is charged to go and find them! Why? Because they matter to the Good Shepherd, Jesus. Jesus speaks about great joy in heaven over the one sinner who repents, and this is who He is talking about. Hold on tightly to that person you know who is lost and struggling, caught in the crane and being dragged away from safety. Join in with your leader and help! Reach out, like Woody! Hold onto that person because, just as Buzz Lightyear mattered to Woody, he or she matters to God!

WORKING TOGETHER AS LEADERS

When you hold on tightly to a wandering sheep, you might be hanging on to a person whom the Lord will raise up to lead as well. The Lord has an incredible imagination when it comes to leadership and who should lead His Church. A quick scan of the New Testament will show that He calls fishermen, a tax collector, a persecuting Pharisee, and even Gentiles. The beauty of the Lord's leadership landscape is that it is so diverse and imaginative!

Leaders also need other people, people who will follow and people who will step up and lead along with them. Some of those people will do things that the leader himself is not capable of doing. They bring skills, abilities, and talents to the table that the team needs in order for ministry to happen. And the beauty of the Church is this: the diversity and complexity of needs are supplied by the Lord through the variety of people who come to faith in Jesus.

The display of differing leadership skills is found in the movie *Toy Story* between Woody and Buzz Lightyear. All seems to be lost. Woody and Buzz are the prisoners of the enemy of all toys, Sid. Trapped in Sid's room, Woody is stuck under a milk crate while Buzz has a firework rocket strapped to his back. But in a powerful and tender moment, Woody builds up Buzz Lightyear and shines the leadership light on him. Woody extols Buzz's virtues, highlights his skills, and empowers him to lead, and that is precisely what Buzz Lightyear does! Moving into high gear, Buzz frees Woody—only to fall into the clutches of Sid, who is bent on shooting off the firework strapped to Buzz's back. And what does Woody do? He leads, of course! Rallying the broken and mutated toys in Sid's room, Woody devises a plan to rescue Buzz. In other words, he embraces his role as a leader who leads with the gifts, talents, and skills he has been given in the circumstances in which he finds himself.[14]

---

14 To view these scenes, watch from 57:14 to 1:01:40 (scene 23, "Buzz, I Can't Do This without You") and 1:01:41 to 1:02:49 (scene 24, "Woody Asks for Help").

The variety of ministry gifts that leaders possess is as wide and vast as the churches that dot the landscape. Some leaders are amazing teachers, while others are tremendous organizers of people. Some leaders are bold proclaimers, while others are gentle shepherds with compassionate and listening ears. No two leaders are alike, but all are necessary and important for the work of the Gospel in the world today. Consider what the apostle Paul wrote to the Church in Corinth:

> I appeal to you, brothers, by the name of our Lord Jesus Christ, that all of you agree, and that there be no divisions among you, but that you be united in the same mind and the same judgment. For it has been reported to me by Chloe's people that there is quarreling among you, my brothers. What I mean is that each one of you says, "I follow Paul," or "I follow Apollos," or "I follow Cephas," or "I follow Christ." Is Christ divided? Was Paul crucified for you? Or were you baptized in the name of Paul? (1 CORINTHIANS 1:10–13)

The apostle Paul reminds the Church in Corinth as well as you and me that our unity depends upon faithfulness to Jesus Christ and not chasing after our own wants, desires, and self-interests. Putting what we want ahead of what the Church needs always leads to friction, fractiousness, and fissure. Paul highlights for the Corinthians that they have been served and blessed by many leaders—Apollos, Cephas, and even himself. But he reminds them that the Church is not about the leader (pastor) but rather the unity of the community that is found in Jesus Christ! Only in that unity can the Church attain to the heights set before it by the Lord.

The Lord raises up specific leaders with specific gifts for specific purposes in the Church. Proclaimers, evangelists, organizers, administrators, compassionate visitors—each serves the Church with a variety of skills for the sake of the Gospel. Take Woody, for example. With Buzz Lightyear moments away from being blown up by Sid, Woody embraces his gifts of leadership to accomplish the rescue of his friend. He organizes the mutated toys of Sid's room, creates a workable plan, directs the various components of the plan, and then executes. The result? Sid is last seen running from his backyard, afraid of his own toys, and Buzz is rescued![15]

In the life of the Church, the Lord raises up specific leaders at precisely the right moments for the Church to accomplish what He has set before it to do. It has been said that the dying words of the Church are "We've never done it that way before." Ultimately, it is a failure to embrace the unique and specific gifts of the leaders that the Lord has given to His Church. The doggish desire to not change, not try something new, or not do something differently is a failure to follow the leaders God appoints for His people. When the mutated toys followed Woody's leadership, Buzz was rescued! How much more can the Church accomplish when it willingly follows the direction of godly leaders?

Now imagine what can happen when pastors and lay leaders work together and use their gifts in a complementary way for the sake of the Gospel! Amazing ministry can unfold. The apostle Paul reminds the Corinthian Church of this very fact. Consider what he tells them:

> What then is Apollos? What is Paul? Servants through whom you believed, as the Lord assigned to each. I planted, Apollos watered, but God gave the growth. So neither he who plants

---

15 To view these scenes, watch from 1:02:50 to 1:04:48 (scene 25, "Wind the Frog") and 1:04:49 to 1:07:57 (scene 26, "Play Nice").

> nor he who waters is anything, but only God who gives the growth. He who plants and he who waters are one, and each will receive his wages according to his labor. For we are God's fellow workers. You are God's field, God's building. (1 CORINTHIANS 3:5–9)

Paul planted (evangelized), Apollos watered (nurtured and taught the Word), but God gave the growth! Paul and Apollos were both blessings to the Corinthian Church. Both men used their gifts of leadership to bless the congregation.

Working together, deferring, yielding, wielding, and exerting gifts of leadership, the Church begins to resemble and fulfill the purpose for which it was established: to share the Gospel of Jesus Christ with the world. Just consider Woody and Buzz for a moment. The only way these two toys were going to be reunited with Andy was by working together. Assisting, helping, and encouraging each other—Woody and Buzz are leaders working together. Only in working together are they able to achieve their goal of reuniting with Andy and the other toys![16]

Whether we realize it or not, leaders who lead are necessary for the well-being of the Church. And these leaders need to work together collaboratively and cooperatively. Although the movie *Toy Story* was a unique, first-of-its-kind computer-animated classic, it also tells the story of leaders who lead. They're not perfect; Woody and Buzz stumble and tumble their own ways, as all leaders do. And yet, each is restored and uses his leadership skills to accomplish the tasks at hand. They are complementary leaders, and when

16 To view these scenes, watch from 1:07:58 to 1:13:09 (scene 27, "The Chase") and 1:13:10 to 1:15:4 (scene 28, "Rocket Power").

they figure that out, they not only accomplish great things but also find friendship and unity.

The same holds true for the Church today. When we allow our pastors and lay leaders to lead, amazing things can happen. Our pastors are called "for such a time as this" (Esther 4:14). Our lay leaders are raised up to use their gifts to assist and bless the ministry of the Church. Today's pastors and lay leaders are no more perfect than Peter, Paul, or Apollos. They will stumble and tumble just like the leaders of the past. But through the blood and righteousness of Jesus Christ, they are restored and given the mantle of leader. They will pursue the lost sheep. They will rejoice over even one who is found. And they will help raise up new leaders in our midst who will bring new ideas, plans, and possibilities to connect people to Jesus. Let's celebrate leaders who lead, because in so doing, we are working together to extend the Gospel of Jesus Christ! In the words of Buzz Lightyear: To infinity and . . . well, you know!

Discussion Questions

1. What is the difference between a lead leader and a leader who leads? Identify the qualities and characteristics of a leader who leads.

2. Create a list of leaders and where you have encountered them. What did they do well? Where was their leadership challenged?

3. Read Psalm 23. What are the characteristics of the care that the Lord provides as our shepherd? What brings you comfort in this psalm?

4. In the movie *Toy Story*, Woody and Buzz Lightyear demonstrate different leadership attributes. What are the leadership attributes demonstrated by Woody? What are the leadership attributes demonstrated by Buzz Lightyear? Which type of leader do you prefer? Why?

5. Read Luke 15. Who are the "lost" in the world today? Why does finding the lost cause celebration in the kingdom of heaven? In the movie *Toy Story*, how does Woody demonstrate this role of shepherd?

6. Although the Church is blessed with a variety of leaders, what is the unifying mission of the Church? How does the Lord use different leaders to guide the Church?

7. Woody and Buzz Lightyear must work together in order to reunite with Andy and the other toys. Why do Church leaders need to work together? Why does the Lord provide the Church with such different leaders?

8. What challenged you in this scene? What did you find affirming to your faith?

TICKET
THE END
CINEMA
MOVIE
TICKET
THE END

SCENE 3

CULTURAL COLLISIONS

FEATURE PRESENTATION

HIDDEN FIGURES

It's not hard to find out where you come from. For a nominal cost, you can order a do-it-yourself DNA kit and find out your heritage. That's exactly what we did one Christmas for my wife, Amy. Amy was adopted and has very little information regarding her birth parents' heritage. She yearned to know where she came from. Additionally, if there is a genetic match or connection with people who have also used a particular DNA testing service, the service will link you together, and voilà! New family members.

To help my wife answer the question of where she came from, we gave her one of these DNA kits for Christmas. With great excitement, she followed the simple steps, dropped it in the mail, and then waited . . . and waited. I guess DNA kits are a pretty popular Christmas present and the processing lab must be overwhelmed in January. Finally, in our mailbox one day was an envelope from the testing company with the results! The answer to *where* was sitting inside a sealed envelope, waiting to be opened by my anxious and excited wife.

From the time my wife was a little girl, she was told by her adoptive parents that her heritage was Italian and English. Despite her fair skin, blue eyes, and red hair, she believed it. In her world, this was her cultural heritage. After all, why wouldn't you believe someone in authority over you when they tell you enough times? But then you grow older, wiser, and more inquisitive. If there is a *where*, maybe there is also a *who*. Maybe, just maybe, there are other people out there who are of my tribe. Maybe there are people who look like me because they are directly connected to me.

Then, with the simple tear of an envelope and a glance at a printed page, my wife's world was changed. She wasn't English or Italian. Rather, the DNA test declared that my wife is Irish, Scottish, Welsh, and Scandinavian. That explained the red hair and blue eyes! Her people had come from these countries. These were now her people, and these were now her cultures.

PEOPLE AND CULTURE

People and culture are two peas in one pod. You cannot have one without the other. People are communal. We cluster together. Sure, there are outliers who flee humanity and isolate themselves in faraway lands. But most people today move to live in closer proximity to one another. Cities are growing, while the outlying rural areas are rapidly depopulating. Global urbanization is on the rise, and as people move to the city centers, they bring with them their cultures.

Culture consists of the unique and identifiable customs, arts, and social structures of an identifiable group of people. Often, culture is expressed in a community's use of language. Even when a language is shared by many culture groups, each group will have their own unique words, phrases, and accents. For example, English is used in the United States, England, and Australia. But put a person from each of these countries into one room, and see how well the communication goes between them!

Culture flows through the rhythms of music, dance, food, dress, values, and religion. In their own unique and wonderful way, these rhythms of culture are beautiful expressions of people who have a shared community and experience. What may be exotic and unusual to me is common and ordinary in another culture. What is odd and out of place to another may be part of the normal rhythm of life that I enjoy within the framework of my culture.

WHEN CULTURES COLLIDE

People are flocking to the urban centers of the world and bringing with them their unique cultures. Globalization has prompted the movement of people all over the world. Regardless of the country, people of different languages, cultures, races, and colors have moved in. You would be hard-pressed today in our Western context to find a monolithic people or culture group. As a result, we are bound to have some cultural collisions. These cultural collisions are expressive, powerful, and at times very painful. People can find themselves pitted against one another—culture is criticized, people are marginalized, and the equality of humankind is pulverized. Instead of the celebration of words such as *culture* and *people*, we are left with the worst understanding of *race*.

Racism. It is ugly, painful, and hurtful. It exudes the worst of a person toward a people group. Words such as *prejudice*, *discrimination*, and *antagonism* are intimately connected to it. Racism cannot be separated from the individual. Racism pushes and prods a person to marginalize and minimize the value and lives of others because of differences in language, culture, and color. And more often than not, the person or people who experience racism are in the minority. Those in the majority who perpetuate racism believe they are superior and weaponize language to minimize the culture and value of those who are different from themselves. Words such as *they* and *them* roll off their tongues with skillful ease, while *we* and *us* lose their unifying quality and are relegated to clarifying difference: "*We* are greater, but *they* are inferior." "It is up to *us* to keep the neighborhood safe from *them*."

Chances are you do not define yourself as a racist. In fact, even the most hardened racists probably don't see themselves in that light. Wearing our own cultural lenses, we see the good things in our language, race, and color. Unfortunately, we can't help but evaluate other cultures in light of our own experience of culture; we can only see other cultures through the cultural lenses we've developed throughout our lives. No analysis of culture happens in a vacuum. We measure and compare the different in light of the known. And since what we know is interwoven into our life story and tends to be affirmed by those who are in authority over us, it almost universally stands as the measuring stick by which all other cultures, languages, nationalities, and colors are measured. Thus, our ability to compare fairly is tainted. We suffer from an intrinsic inability to be objective.

CULTURAL COLLISIONS ARE NOT NEW

A well-known cultural collision happened on the Day of Pentecost in the year Jesus was crucified and rose from the dead. The disciples were all together when the sound of a rushing wind filled the house. Tongues of fire separated and appeared above their heads, and immediately they were able to speak in other languages as the Spirit gave them ability.

> Now there were dwelling in Jerusalem Jews, devout men from every nation under heaven. And at this sound the multitude came together, and they were bewildered, because each one was hearing them [the disciples] speak in his own language. And they were amazed and astonished, saying, "Are not all these who are speaking Galileans? And how is it that we hear, each of us in his own native language? Parthians and Medes and Elamites and residents of Mesopotamia, Judea and Cappadocia, Pontus and Asia, Phrygia and Pamphylia, Egypt and the parts of Libya belonging to Cyrene, and visitors from Rome, both Jews and proselytes, Cretans and Arabians—we hear them telling in our own tongues the mighty works of God." And all were amazed and perplexed, saying to one another, "What does this mean?" But others mocking said, "They are filled with new wine." (ACTS 2:5–13)

Jewish pilgrims from a variety of lands gathered in Jerusalem to celebrate the festival of Pentecost. Although culturally diverse and linguistically divided, they were indivisible and uniform in faith and practice as Jews. They were the majority, standing around together in wonder and awe at this Spirit-driven event.

What was their response to the Spirit-infused disciples of Jesus? Surprise. Astonishment. Bewilderment. How could these Galileans speak in the listeners' native tongues? There was a cultural collision happening in Jerusalem. The gathered Jews of the diaspora were struggling to accept that Galileans were perfectly speaking their respective languages. Why was this so unbelievable? Because the

Galilean dialect was considered peculiar, with swallowed syllables and mushy gutturals. Even the Talmud pokes fun at the Galilean dialect. Yet these Galileans were speaking plainly and clearly in the respective languages of these "devout men."

There could only be two reactions: patience to see the miracle unfold or ridicule and dismissiveness. And therein lies the cultural collision. Could another culture group receive the Holy Spirit in a supernatural way? Or was that impossible simply because those men were Galileans? Were the disciples Spirit-filled or drunk? Through what lenses would these "devout men" view Jesus' followers as they watched the miracle unfolding before their eyes?

We find out after Peter's bold and direct sermon. "So those who received his word were baptized, and there were added that day about three thousand souls" (Acts 2:41). But how many were listening? How many continued to believe that these Galileans were drunk or out of their minds? How many refused to see this moment through different lenses and accept that men from this different culture and different race could be filled with the Holy Spirit and proclaim the Word of God in all of its truth and purity? The text is silent. But if we understand the nature of sin and divisiveness, we can be sure there were plenty who chose to ignore (at best) or mock and ridicule (at worst) these Spirit-filled disciples of Jesus who were deemed culturally inferior to their listening audience.

THE EDGE OF COLLISION

In 2016, director Theodore Melfi and 20th Century Fox brought to the big screen an adapted screenplay about three Black women who were integral to the NASA program in the early 1960s. The relatively untold story of Katherine Johnson (played by Taraji P. Henson),

Dorothy Vaughan (played by Octavia Spencer), and Mary Jackson (played by Janelle Monáe) comes to life with all of their brains and brilliance. But the movie also brings to light the important struggle of racism and cultural collisions—collisions that in large part are still with us today.[17]

Many of you reading this may have never been pulled over by a police officer while driving your car. For the most part, you have lived your life following God's Word and mindful of the civil laws that are in place. And if you have been pulled over by a police officer, you were more than likely aware of your civil transgression and awaited the penalty for your infraction of the law. But what if you were pulled over even though you had broken no law? What if you were pulled over simply because you were different—different sex? different skin color? different race? To what level would your anxiety rise? Would you be able to control your anger and your fear?

In the opening scene of *Hidden Figures*, the three women—Katherine, Dorothy, and Mary—find themselves stranded on a lonely Virginia road with a broken-down car. As they try to figure out their mechanical dilemma, fear and anger begin to bubble up when they see a police car coming their way with the lights a-blazing and siren roaring. They know that when this police officer gets out of his car, their problems could multiply. The White police officer exits his car, clenching his baton—three well-dressed, professional Black women with a broken-down car warrant the police officer approaching with his baton? But that is what he does. And when he speaks, his tone is superior, disrespectful, and clearly racially charged.

---

17 *Hidden Figures*, directed by Theodore Melfi (2016; Los Angeles, CA: 20th Century Fox Home Entertainment, 2017), DVD.

On the edge of a cultural collision, the ball is in the police officer's court. He asks the three women for identification. The anxiety level is increasing by the second. But when the women identify themselves as people who work for NASA, who "do a great deal of the calculating, getting our rockets into space," the racially charged moment turns into something very different. The officer is clearly dumbfounded that NASA employed Black people, and women at that! After all, it is the 1960s! And yet the women gracefully diffuse the police officer's overt racism with the gentle words: "There are quite a few women working in the space program."

For this police officer, the lens of nationalism is stronger than the lens of racism. At the time, the United States had fallen behind the Soviet Union in the race to space. The Russians had launched the satellite Sputnik 1 on October 4, 1957, and the thought that the United States was losing to their international rival was unpalatable to the American people. The desire for American success was a far stronger pull than the divisiveness of color or culture at this moment. Instead of hindering or hurting, the officer's attitude changes to pride and helpfulness. He wants to engage these women in a meaningful way. But what can he do? While he ponders this question, Dorothy is able to fix the car; after all, she is a capable and talented woman of color. He offers them a police escort some sixteen miles down the country road with lights a-blazing and siren roaring—but this time helping the very women he initially suspected. As Mary thunders down the road behind the police car, she exclaims to the other women, "Three Negro women is chasing a White police officer down the highway in Hampton, Virginia, 1961. Ladies, that there is a God-ordained miracle!"[18]

Jesus was quite aware of the cultural edge. He never backed away from it and often brought His listeners right up to the precipice. One time, a lawyer approached Jesus to put Him to the test, asking, "Teacher, what shall I do to inherit eternal life?" (Luke 10:25). Why is it that the lawyers, Pharisees, and other religious leaders couldn't figure out that Jesus was always multiple steps ahead of them? Why is it that they couldn't figure out that Jesus would take them to the cultural edge and challenge them to rethink how they viewed His kingdom? What follows in the parable is familiar and challenging.

> [Jesus] said to him, "What is written in the Law? How do you read it?" And he answered, "You shall love the Lord your God with all your heart and with all your soul and with all your strength and with all your mind, and your neighbor as yourself." And He said to him, "You have answered correctly; do this, and you will live."
>
> But he, desiring to justify himself, said to Jesus, "And who is my neighbor?" Jesus replied, "A man was going down from Jerusalem to Jericho, and he fell among robbers, who stripped him and beat him and departed, leaving him half dead. Now by chance a priest was going down that road, and when he saw him he passed by on the other side. So likewise a Levite, when he came to the place and saw him, passed by on the other side. But a Samaritan, as he journeyed, came to where he was, and when he saw him, he had compassion. He went to him and bound up his wounds,

18 To view this scene, watch from 2:55 to 6:52 (scene 2).

> pouring on oil and wine. Then he set him on his own animal and brought him to an inn and took care of him. And the next day he took out two denarii and gave them to the innkeeper, saying, 'Take care of him, and whatever more you spend, I will repay you when I come back.' Which of these three, do you think, proved to be a neighbor to the man who fell among the robbers?" He said, "The one who showed him mercy." And Jesus said to him, "You go, and do likewise." (LUKE 10:26–37)

Love. Love the Lord your God, and love your neighbor as yourself. The summation of the Law, both vertically and horizontally. And yet, when we look at the parable of Jesus, those who should have had the most intimate knowledge of the Law (the priest and the Levite) seemed to be ignorant (at best) or dismissive (at worst) of the law of love. The priest and the Levite shared culture and faith with the battered and broken man on the side of the road, but they wouldn't demonstrate relational care by helping the one in need. Instead, they went out of their way to pass the broken man on the other side of the road.

Which brings us to the Samaritan. Here is the cultural edge. The Samaritan would have been perceived by the inquisitive lawyer as an adherent of a false religion and in a place he didn't belong (outside of Samaria). The Samaritan walked the same road as the priest and the Levite. He encountered the same broken and battered man. But when he looked upon the man in distress—this man who was religiously and culturally different from himself—we are told he had compassion. The Samaritan understood the law of love. The Samaritan danced on the cultural edge and fell to the side of help, care, and sacrifice. Martin Luther wrote this on the topic of our neighbor:

> Finally, no creature toward which you should practice love is nobler than your neighbor. He is not a devil, not a lion or a bear or a wolf, not a stone or a log. He is a living creature very much like you. There is nothing living on earth that is more pleasant, more lovable, more helpful, kinder, more comforting, or more necessary. Besides, he is naturally suited for a civilized and social existence. Thus nothing could be regarded as worthier of love in the whole universe than our neighbor.[19]

This is the same cultural edge we are brought to every day when we view, encounter, and interact with people who are racially and culturally different from us. The Western context becomes more and more diverse with each passing day. The lack of unity in language and cultural expression makes it harder for us to keep up with the diversity and differences between people. And yet, according to Jesus, these are our neighbors. Am I willing to sacrifice time, talent, and treasure to assist and advance my neighbor's life and well-being? Am I willing to drop my pretenses and listen to the story of the battered, the broken, and the marginalized? Am I willing, like Martin Luther, to embrace the notion that this person seemingly different from myself is actually very much like me?

Ask yourself: Will you pass by on the other side of the road? Or will you engage with a heart and mind that is sacrificial and merciful? Will you allow your heart to be turned, like the police officer, and help your neighbor? Will you diffuse tension with

19 Martin Luther, Luther's Works, vol. 27 (St. Louis: Concordia Publishing House, 1964), 58.

grace, like the three women? Will you show compassion, like the Samaritan, and bind the wounds and carry the burden of the neighbor? If you do, you will have avoided the cultural collision and embraced the law of love.

CROSSING THE CULTURAL DIVIDE

There are moments in life when we are confronted with a clearly defined division: I am here, and you are there. These are my people, and those are your people. To cross over and stand with the other side creates discomfort and can make others feel uneasy. This divide is usually defined by skin color or language—a racial division. But divisions can also be more subtle, such as with religion, education, food, clothing, music, or dance. These divisions are often tossed into the bucket of culture. But they can create a profound tension when we wander into places where we are perceived not to belong racially or culturally.

The movie *Hidden Figures* clearly demonstrates such a divide in a scene when NASA employees meet the astronauts. All those working at Langley for NASA are gathered outside of the airplane hangars to greet those who have been selected as the pioneering astronauts for the United States. Alan Shepard, Scott Carpenter, Walter Schirra, and John Glenn get out of military Jeeps to the applause and cheers of the gathered crowd. But there is something quite striking about those assembled. In front of the place where the Jeeps stop are all the White NASA engineers and office workers; to the distant right of that group are all the Black NASA employees, including Katherine, Dorothy, and Mary.

After the astronauts greet the White workers, they are told by the coordinator that the time for greetings has concluded; the agenda has them moving on to see the base and the work that is going on to get them into outer space. All the astronauts follow the directive—except for John Glenn. John Glenn exclaims, "We haven't shaken all the hands yet," and walks toward the group of Black women, who are separated from the crowd. What follows is the crossing of the cultural divide. John Glenn demonstrates sincere and authentic engagement with these women. He talks with them. He listens to them. He genuinely engages with and values them as equals. And these women are genuinely touched. They reciprocate with words of pride and unity of spirit.[20]

Crossing the cultural divide is Christlike. Early in the Gospel of John, we find Jesus traveling from Judea back to Galilee. However, the Gospel of John has a very interesting turn of phrase: Jesus "had to pass through Samaria" (John 4:4). Jesus was a Jew. Most Jews despised Samaritans, and vice versa. When traveling between Galilee and Jerusalem, Jewish travelers would cross the Jordan River, travel down the eastern side of the river, and then cross back over simply to avoid Samaria. There was history between the two peoples—lots of history. And that history was littered with bad blood and bitterness. As a result, there was strong mutual antagonism between them.

But Jesus "had to pass through Samaria." Jesus had to cross the cultural divide. Jesus was on a mission. Race, culture, language, skin color, and the like would not stop Jesus from going where He needed to go and accomplishing what He needed to do. When Jesus and His disciples came to the outskirts of the village named Sychar, Jesus sent the disciples into the town to buy food while He went and sat by Jacob's well. Jesus needed to cross the cultural

20 To view this scene, watch from 36:06 to 37:45 (scene 10).

divide. While sitting by the well, Jesus encountered a "woman from Samaria" (John 4:7) who had come to the well to draw water. With a simple request, "Give Me a drink" (John 4:7), Jesus crossed the cultural divide.

Jesus was a Jew. The woman was a Samaritan. Jesus was a man. She was a woman. Race, culture, and gender are traversed with four simple words: "Give Me a drink." And then a lengthy and heartfelt conversation unfolded. But Jesus was not bound by the prejudices of His time and place. Rather, He crossed the cultural divide and engaged the woman intellectually and spiritually. She was lifted from her place of brokenness to a place of spiritual freedom.

In their exchange at the well, the woman said to Jesus, "I know that Messiah is coming (He who is called Christ). When He comes, He will tell us all things" (John 4:25). Jesus responded, "I who speak to you am He" (John 4:26). This Samaritan woman became the recipient of a simple truth right from the source: this Jesus is the Messiah! Jesus traveled across the cultural divide to deliver to her living water and eternal life. No racial or cultural boundaries could stop Jesus from blessing this woman!

But there is more. The Gospel of John goes on to tell us that at precisely that moment, the disciples came back to the well. When they saw Jesus talking with the woman, they were dumbstruck. Jesus had sent them into the town to buy food. He sent them to engage Samaritans in their village and at their shops. He sent them to talk with Samaritans, and He knew that was probably going to make them culturally uncomfortable. Jesus sent them to cross the cultural divide as well!

When they returned, they found Jesus not only crossing the cultural divide but also talking with a woman! The Gospel of John says that "no one said, 'What do you seek?' or, 'Why are

You talking with her?'" (4:27). It would have been within reason to ask Jesus why He spoke with this Samaritan woman. Jewish law prohibited a rabbi from talking with a woman in public, and Jesus was their rabbi (or teacher). But the disciples refrained from such questions. Although Jesus often was unconventional as a rabbi, He always had a reason for doing what He did. And in this moment, Jesus was showing the disciples by His own actions and by sending them to the Samaritan town for food that it is not only right but also necessary to cross the cultural divide for the sake of the Gospel.

The racial and cultural divide seems to be growing in our Western context. Despite our efforts to make progress and raise awareness, the world seems more divided now than ever. It is not uncommon for people to (metaphorically) "cross over the Jordan and travel on the eastern side" in order to avoid encountering or crossing into unfamiliar (or unwelcoming) places. Yet this is precisely where Jesus would have us go! Ask yourself: Am I willing to open myself up to the unknown and encounter my fellow person in his or her cultural and racial context that may make me feel uncomfortable because I am out of my familiar surroundings? Am I willing to listen to his or her heart song and respond with patience, care, and concern in his or her context?

John Glenn left behind the racial and cultural expectations of his day to engage the Black women right where they stood. His focus was on them—their excitement, contributions, and brilliance. Jesus left behind the racial and cultural expectations of the Jews to engage a Samaritan woman at the well and reveal His glory. Are you ready to leave behind the racial and cultural expectations of today to be a voice of love and compassion so that you may witness to the power of the Gospel of Jesus Christ to those who are not like you?

WHEN CULTURES COLLIDE

There are moments when cultural collisions are unavoidable. These collisions can be sharp and edgy. These collisions can make those in the majority feel uncomfortable because they are forced to hear words they don't want to hear and see things they don't want to see. They are drawn out of their relatively comfortable and defined world and faced with the discomfort, pain, and distress of someone who is racially and culturally different from them. How you see and interact with the world around you is challenged by how other people see and experience that same world. But what if water fountains, coffee pots, bathrooms, and seats on a public bus were race-specific? What if you were relegated to use only those things that were assigned to you because of the color of your skin or the language you spoke?

The movie *Hidden Figures* is set in a time when this was the reality for Black Americans. Designated bathrooms and water fountains. Seats set apart in the back of the bus. Public schools segregated by race. Many opportunities simply were not available to Black people because of the color of their skin. Katherine Johnson experiences all of this in a powerful scene in the movie. Due to segregation, she has to walk over half a mile each way in order to use a "Colored bathroom." The cultural collision is set into motion when Katherine is running to and from the bathroom on a rain-soaked day; her boss, Al Harrison (played by Kevin Costner), is furious that his brilliant mathematician is seemingly always missing from their workroom when he needs trajectory figures from her.

When Katherine arrives back in the work room, dripping wet from her mile circuit to and from the "Colored bathroom," Al Harrison confronts her: "Where the hell have you been? Everywhere I look you are not where I need you to be. It's not my imagination. Now where the hell do you go every day?" The room filled with White mathematicians and administrators falls uncomfortably silent. Katherine's answer is simple: "To the bathroom, sir." Al Harrison is incensed! "The bathroom? . . . For forty minutes a day? What are you doing there?" It never occurs to Al Harrison that "her" bathroom is not easily accessible or close by. He views the world through the lens of accomplishing the task of space flight for America and has put aside the lenses of race and culture.

And then the collision occurs. Katherine exclaims: "There is no bathroom for me here. . . . There are no Colored bathrooms in this building." The emotional, racial, and cultural pain comes pouring out and cannot be stopped. The litany is cried out: "I can't use one of the handy bikes. . . . You don't pay Coloreds enough to afford pearls. . . . I work like a dog day and night living off of coffee from a pot none of you want to touch!" In that moment, you can feel the pain, anger, and hurt of the one who has been marginalized. And what about Al Harrison and the remainder of the White work team? The uncomfortable and recognizable guilt and shame that comes with realizing racism within oneself is powerful. After Katherine leaves the room, Al Harrison walks over to the coffee pot reserved for Katherine. He looks around and then sheepishly removes the "Colored" label from the pot.[21]

When cultural collisions happen, we all feel uncomfortable. Why? There is real tension, pain, hurt, and anger. Emotions are

21 To view this scene, watch from 57:35 to 1:00:52 (scene 15).

raw, and the sense of injustice is overwhelming, especially for the one who has experienced the racism and marginalization. And yet, when we look at the ministry of Jesus, we find similar collisions. In the Gospel of Matthew, Jesus withdraws to the district of Tyre and Sidon (Matthew 15:21–28). Traveling north and east of Galilee, Jesus has ventured into Phoenician territory—pagan territory.

The Gospel of Matthew displays a side of Jesus and His disciples that makes us a little uncomfortable. Just what does a cultural collision look like for Jesus and His disciples?

> And behold, a Canaanite woman from that region came out and was crying, "Have mercy on me, O Lord, Son of David; my daughter is severely oppressed by a demon." But He did not answer her a word. And His disciples came and begged Him, saying, "Send her away, for she is crying out after us." He answered, "I was sent only to the lost sheep of the house of Israel." But she came and knelt before Him, saying, "Lord, help me." And He answered, "It is not right to take the children's bread and throw it to the dogs." She said, "Yes, Lord, yet even the dogs eat the crumbs that fall from their masters' table." Then Jesus answered her, "O woman, great is your faith! Be it done for you as you desire." And her daughter was healed instantly. (MATTHEW 15:22–28)

The tension is thick, and the cultures are slamming against each other. We have come to expect the disciples to avoid difficult moments of ministry. These are the same men who wanted Jesus to disperse the crowds when it was late and there was no food to eat by the Sea of Galilee. But we do not expect Jesus to say things like, "I was sent only to the lost sheep of the house of Israel" (Matthew 15:24), and "It is not right to take the children's bread and throw it to the dogs" (Matthew 15:26). You would think this pagan, Canaanite woman would have gotten the message: "You're not My people. Go away!" At least, that is what Jesus appears to be saying! But what was Jesus up to? Clearly, the loving Savior of the world was not discarding this Canaanite woman and her need because she wasn't Jewish. No, Jesus was setting the stage for a teachable moment—to demonstrate to the disciples (and you and me) how we can overcome our cultural collisions to demonstrate love, compassion, and mercy.

Look how this unfolds: children versus dogs, bread versus crumbs, Jew versus Gentile. Therein lies the collision. And yet this Canaanite woman turned the table (and Jesus' own words) and demonstrated a grace and faithfulness that far exceeded the disciples' racial and cultural anxiety. "Yes, Lord, yet even the dogs eat the crumbs that fall from their masters' table" (Matthew 15:27). She doesn't argue the racial inequality but rather addresses the overwhelming, awe-inspiring grace that God alone can demonstrate in this moment. Even a crumb of God's mercy is sufficient for her daughter. Even a simple word from Jesus can make her well. And Jesus' response? "O woman, great is your faith! Be it done for you as you desire" (Matthew 15:28).

A word, an action, a moment of reserved patience and care can change a collision into an embrace. In this moment, Jesus demonstrated to us that even in the cultural maelstrom, there can be grace, mercy, and compassion. Hearts can be softened, cultures can be embraced, and attitudes can be changed. After Katherine's encounter with Al Harrison, the unthinkable occurs. In 1960s Virginia, where segregation and separation was the law of the day, Al Harrison is found in the hallway with a crowbar knocking down the "Colored Ladies Room" sign. As a mix of people watches him remove the sign, Al Harrison exclaims, "There you have it. No more Colored restrooms. No more White restrooms. Just plain old toilets."[22] The cultural collision with Katherine softened Al Harrison and prompted him to remove the racial barriers in their workplace. The common goal of getting Americans into space as well as Katherine sharing her experience shattered the lens of racism that divided them.

No matter who we are or where we are from, we each see the world through racial and cultural lenses. You are aware of your heritage, culture, skin color, and language. As you look at the world around you, these lenses filter what you see. Jesus and the disciples saw the woman as Canaanite and pagan. Al Harrison saw Katherine as a Black woman. But Jesus chose to see the Canaanite woman as a child of God with great faith. Al Harrison learned to see Katherine as a brilliant mathematician whose job was compromised by racism. Through what lenses do you see the world? Are you willing to set them aside to view the world differently?

WHEN LOVE AND GRACE PREVAIL

When we stop viewing other people based on divisions and differences and instead see them through the lens of God's love and grace, great things can happen and new relationships can form. Rather than being separated and divided by our skin color or language, we see how God unites us and all of our uniqueness in a beautiful tapestry of culture. God has uniquely and wonderfully blessed each person with skills and abilities that complement others and help to grow society. In the movie *Hidden Figures*,

---

22 To view this scene, watch from 1:00:53 to 1:00:55 (scene 16).

one such beautiful moment occurs when Al Harrison must show John Glenn and the military team the math that determines the re-entry location for Glenn's spacecraft. But Al is not the person to demonstrate the math. Rather, it is Katherine, a brilliant Black woman who will contribute in such a mighty and profound way by providing accurate and precise coordinates for John Glenn's potential return to earth. Al hands Katherine the chalk to show the math. A White man handing a Black woman the chalk—the beautiful tapestry of God's creation working together in harmony.[23]

What is possible when culture and race are transcended by God's love and grace? The Book of Acts tells the wonderful account of Philip and the Ethiopian. The angel of the Lord sent Philip south of Jerusalem toward Gaza. When he arrived,

> there was an Ethiopian, a eunuch, a court official of Candace, queen of the Ethiopians, who was in charge of all her treasure. He had come to Jerusalem to worship and was returning, seated in his chariot, and he was reading the prophet Isaiah. And the Spirit said to Philip, "Go over and join this chariot." So Philip ran to him and heard him reading Isaiah the prophet and asked, "Do you understand what you are reading?" And he said, "How can I, unless someone guides me?" And he invited Philip to come up and sit with him. (ACTS 8:27–31)

"And he invited Philip." Philip was a Galilean Jew. The other man was an Ethiopian court official. Philip was an ordinary man. The Ethiopian was a man of importance and stature. But God's love and grace prevailed. A conversation was shared. Faith was

23 To view this scene, watch 1:18:57 to 1:22:45 (scene 20).

demonstrated. And a Baptism was performed in the midst of a cultural and racial collision in which faith in Jesus was the uniting thread. (Read Acts 8:32–40 for the rest of the story.)

Cultural collisions happen around us every single day. Race, color, language, food, dance, dress, customs, traditions—if we try not to bump into different races and cultures, we might have to confine ourselves to our homes and never open the door, turn on the TV, or view social media. But God has blessed the world with colorful, vibrant, and diverse people. As brothers and sisters in Christ, it is our duty and delight to reflect the all-encompassing love and grace of Jesus, which compels us to follow our Savior and take to heart His mandate: "Go therefore and make disciples of all nations, baptizing them in the name of the Father and of the Son and of the Holy Spirit" (Matthew 28:19). That's right, go and make disciples of *all* nations—all colors, all cultures, all languages, all people!

Discussion Questions

1. What are your cultural origins? What unique traditions and customs do you observe from your culture? How many generations are you removed from your countries of origin?

2. How do you define racism? Through what lenses do you view other cultures? What cultures make you uncomfortable? Why?

3. What was the cultural collision that took place on Pentecost? Why was it so surprising that the disciples of Jesus could speak in the variety of languages that were present in Jerusalem? What were the two responses from the gathered Jews?

4. What is the law of love? How did the Good Samaritan demonstrate the law of love? How did the women and the police officer demonstrate the law of love to one another? How can you demonstrate the law of love across cultures today?

5. When have you crossed the cultural divide and entered into a Samaria? How did you feel as the outsider in a different culture? How did you demonstrate grace and humility? How did you grow?

6. Think of a time in your life when your heart was changed by the needs of a person culturally different from yourself. How did you demonstrate the love and compassion of Jesus in that moment? What opportunity of care were you able to seize upon?

7. In the movie *Hidden Figures*, Al Harrison demonstrates the ability to view life differently in order to accomplish the task of getting an American into space. Through what lenses do you see the world? How can you be a Philip to a person of a different race or culture?

8. What challenged you in this scene? What did you find affirming to your faith?

TICKET
THE END
CINEMA
MOVIE
TICKET
THE END

SCENE 4

DON'T BE A SUPERHERO

FEATURE PRESENTATION

CAPTAIN AMERICA

THE FIRST AVENGER

It never ceases to amaze me that simple things in life can serve as anchor points—that upon hearing, smelling, or seeing something, we can be transported back through time to our distant past. Hear a certain song, and immediately you are brought back to your wedding day or a special time in high school. Have a fragrance tickle your nose, and be taken back to your grandmother's kitchen when you were a child. See an old television show on YouTube, and be reminded of those simpler days when that was the most important thing to watch when you got home from school.

Every so often, I want to travel to my childhood, and the easiest way to do so is to search on YouTube for the old television show *Batman*. I am not talking about one of the many animated cartoons nor one of the score of movies that have been made from 1989 to the present. Rather, I am referring to the classic television show that ran from January 12, 1966, to March 14, 1968, on the American Broadcasting Company (ABC). Starring Adam West as Batman and Burt Ward as Robin, each week the superheroes were confronted with villains such as the Joker, Penguin, Catwoman, and the Riddler. By the time I was introduced to the show, it was in syndication and ran every day from 4:00 to 5:00 p.m. on a local television network.

This show is one of those anchor points for my life. When I hear the theme song and see the actors, I am transported back to my parents' house in Spotswood, New Jersey: plaid couch and shag carpet, a wall covered in shelves filled with books, an easy chair with a footstool, and in the middle of it all, the television playing *Batman.* To be sure, the show was hokey, the costumes flamboyant, and the acting a little over the top. But there he was in living color—my favorite superhero, Batman.

THE WHAT AND WHY OF HEROES

Whether we realize it or not, in our lives we all have characters or people that we have set apart in the category of *hero.* Heroes are characters or people we admire or even idealize because of their courage, achievements, noble qualities, or brave acts. Heroes will demonstrate great bravery or leadership in the moment of adversity. Heroes place other people before themselves for the sake of the well-being of others. Heroes are the embodiment of the very best of humankind. Heroes inspire us to dream and motivate us to be better people and better citizens.

As a result, we find ourselves looking for heroes all around us. Baseball fields and basketball courts, stages and theater screens, battlefields and books—all are places where we search for inspiration and motivation. That is why heroes can be living or dead, real or fictitious. Martin Luther can be viewed as a hero for his staunch defense of the Gospel, and he continues to bring inspiration to millions of Christians through his writings that live on well beyond his mortal life. Batman, an entirely fictitious character, is also considered a hero by many and is brought to life by comic books, animated shows, and live-action movies because of his unyielding defense of the helpless and the marginalized. Is Martin Luther a hero? Is Batman a hero? That is for you to consider and answer for yourself.

Whether they are in the pages of history, playing in athletic competitions, contributing to the arts, or entirely fictitious characters, heroes display what we hope and desire for ourselves, such as intelligence, strength, courage, determination, faithfulness, and leadership. Where you see weakness in yourself, you find strength in your hero. Where you find shortcomings in your life, you find the embodiment of excellence in your hero. Simply put, heroes represent the best in humankind and inspire us to be better people.

BIBLE HEROES?

Even within the framework of the Church, we seek to identify and uphold biblical people in the position of hero. A simple online search will yield a plethora of books (both children's and adult) with the word *hero* somewhere in the title and connected to someone from the Bible. And why not? The people of the Bible are inspirational, faithful, and driven by divine purpose to fulfill God's calling in their lives.

The biblical hero is a *real* hero. What do I mean by that? Biblical heroes are powerful and relatable: not only do they live out God's calling and fulfill divine purpose, but also (other than Jesus Christ) they are flawed and have shortcomings. That's right: shortcomings! They are more like us than we realize! Flawed, sinful, fractured, and striving to live according to God's Word and share God's grace, the people of Scripture look and sound like us. If you were to do a quick scan of Sunday School materials or children's Bible videos about heroes, names such as Abraham, Moses, Samson, and Jonah are at the front of the line. What Sunday School curriculum hasn't upheld these men as heroes? And yet, they are very similar to us in our walks of faith.

Let's take a closer look. Abram was called by God, followed God's lead, and became the father of God's chosen people, a great nation (see Genesis 12–25), and that's very heroic. But Abram encountered some bumps along the way. For example, when famine came upon his land, he sojourned to Egypt for food. While there, he tried to pass off his wife, Sarai, as his sister to preserve his own life, putting Sarai in danger when the pharaoh took her as a wife (see Genesis 12:10–20). If you are married, I doubt you would be quick to follow in Abram's sandals with this stunt. This was an epic failure of faith! Somehow, Abram concluded that the God who led him this far would not protect him in his time of need. Not very heroic. But his breakdown of faith-filled confidence is relatable.

What about Moses? He may be the pinnacle of Old Testament heroes. The Books of Exodus, Leviticus, Numbers, and Deuteronomy are filled with the story of his life and faith. Protected from birth, raised in Pharaoh's court, spokesman of God, deliverer of the plagues in Egypt, divider of the Red Sea, giver of the Ten Commandments, leader of the children of Israel to the Promised Land—now this is the stuff heroes are made of! But Moses also had a temper. Early in the story, Moses lost that temper and killed an Egyptian for abusing a Hebrew (Exodus 2:11–15). That's not very heroic! And I suspect most of us struggle in relating to this moral failing. But we have moral failings too, and those failings have consequences. He's more relatable than we think.

Surely Samson is a Bible hero without flaw! Well, not so fast. Although God chose Samson from birth to be set apart as a Nazirite,[24] and Samson could tear apart a lion with his bare hands (Judges 14:6), his life was rather entangled in love affairs and foolish decisions. He violated his Nazirite vows, specialized in liaisons with Philistine women of questionable repute, and continually disrespected his parents. Finally, Samson was blinded by his passion for Delilah. She cut his hair, which drained him of his God-given strength. Samson was bound as a prisoner, had his eyes gouged out (ugh!), and died when he brought the building down around his captors. Not necessarily a hero we can easily relate to in our daily life! It's safe to say that Samson wasn't perfect!

But all hope is not lost—certainly the prophet Jonah won't let us down. After all, he was the great deliverer of the message of repentance to Nineveh, and the people of Nineveh listened and repented of their sinful ways! Truly a success story of a faithful servant of God. But before that, Jonah was gripped by fear or anger (or both!), disobeyed God, and fled the other way (Jonah 1:1–3). He was thrown overboard while attempting to flee the scene of God's call. Then "the LORD appointed a great fish to swallow up Jonah. And Jonah was in the belly of the fish three days and three nights" (Jonah 1:17). We are told that after Jonah's lengthy prayer (I think I would be praying too!), "the LORD spoke to the fish, and it vomited Jonah out upon the dry land" (Jonah 2:10). Okay, the Bible can be a little gross from time to time. Then Jonah goes to Nineveh. The people repent, and he has prophetic success! The heroic prophet!

---

24 Nazirites were people who made vows to God, setting themselves apart for a time. Numbers 6:1–21 details Nazirite vows, which included not cutting their hair, not drinking alcohol, and not touching a dead body. Usually these vows were temporary, but Samson was to be a Nazirite from birth. (See *The Lutheran Study Bible* notes on Numbers 6:1–21; Numbers 6:2; Numbers 6:4.)

But then Jonah pouts. The story ends with a pouting hero. Not very heroic. In fact, very broken and pitiable—and very relatable. We can understand disappointment and anger with God. We all can throw a good pity party every now and again.

HEROES ARE HERE TO STAY

Although heroes are fractured and flawed, they are still able to inspire us to dream and motivate us to be better. Heroes are important because they highlight the very best in humankind even while revealing their warts and blemishes. But don't take my word for it—just look at the world around us! Athletes, entertainers, and historical figures are embraced and adored in all their grandeur *and* brokenness. The heroes of fiction have all followed suit! Despite their super strength, speed, intelligence, and abilities, fictional heroes are wrapped in fractured and flawed packages. While a fictional character could be presented as perfect, that is not real, relatable, or honest.

We see this with the proliferation of superhero movies that have made their way to the big screen, beginning in 1978 with the release of *Superman* and stretching to today's Avengers and Justice League movies. These movies are coming in bunches and building upon one another. People are hungering and thirsting for heroes, and Hollywood is ready to deliver the fantastic and otherworldly heroes that we seek. I think it is safe to say that heroes are here to stay.

If heroes are here to stay, what makes a good hero? What are the benchmarks that we look for in such a person? Movies can highlight those things that are most appealing to people today—after all, Hollywood is making a product that needs to be sold, and people will buy what they want and what they need. And what we need is to encounter real heroes who inspire us to be better.

THE UNLIKELY HERO

In 2011, director Joe Johnston and Marvel Studios brought *Captain America: The First Avenger* to the big screen. The movie features the comic book superhero Captain America (aka Steve Rogers), played by Chris Evans. In the movie, it's March 1942, and the world is at war. The Germans have a secret agency called Hydra led by a villainous leader, Red Skull. (With a name like *Red Skull*, how could you not be evil?) His evil and diabolical plans can throw the balance of the war toward the Nazis. Meanwhile, the US government is working on a secret plan to create a battalion of super soldiers.[25]

Enter our would-be hero, Steve Rogers. But he does not look the part. He is a ninety-eight-pound weakling who suffers from asthma, sinusitis, chronic colds, high blood pressure, heart palpitations, and fatigue, not to mention that he has suffered from scarlet fever and rheumatic fever, has a nervous disorder, and has a family history of diabetes! Our hero is not off to a good start. We meet Steve Rogers trying to enlist in the United States Army, where he is summarily dismissed by the medical board. What a shock! And this was not his first attempt! But he is our hero, and heroes do not give up.

Next, Steve Rogers visits the World Exposition of Tomorrow with his friend James "Bucky" Barnes, who is shipping out for England the next day to serve as a sergeant in the Army. While at

---

25 *Captain America: The First Avenger*, directed by Joe Johnston (2011; Hollywood, CA: Paramount Pictures, 2011), DVD.

the exposition, Steve Rogers tries to enlist again. This time, he meets Dr. Abraham Erskine. Dr. Erskine is the lead medical researcher for the Strategic Scientific Reserve, the elite scientific group working on the Super Soldier project. Before Dr. Erskine approves him, Steve must first answer a character question. Dr. Erskine asks, "So, you want to . . . kill some Nazis?" In fact, he asks the question a few times. Only upon receiving the right answer does he approve Steve Rogers to join the Army and become a part of the Super Soldier Program.[26]

What exactly is a character question? The question asked of Steve Rogers was critical in revealing his heart. What motivates a sickly ninety-eight-pound man to try to join the Army over and over again? Is it to act like a big man? Is it to exact his own form of justice? In his answer, we begin to see the character of our hero. Steve Rogers says, "I don't want to kill anyone. I don't like bullies. I don't care where they're from." The heart and character of Steve Rogers are justice and fairness. There is no room in his world for bullies and those who take advantage of others.

And so his training begins. Steve Rogers is a small man in a large world. He cannot keep up; he is outmatched by the physicality of military training. But he has the character of a hero. He has the heart of a man who puts other people first, values life, and seeks justice. He demonstrates an emotional intelligence that sets him apart from other physically superior soldiers. Dr. Erskine has chosen wisely; he anoints Steve Rogers to become Captain America.[27]

---

26 To view this scene, watch from 12:55 to 17:15 (scene 2).

27 To view this scene, watch from 19:45 to 27:53 (scenes 3–4).

ANOINTED

A hero is not self-appointed. A hero *is* because others see and affirm that person's heroicness. The hero is set apart from the rest; he or she is different in both physicality and intellectual capacity. Heroes have a strong sense of justice and righteousness. And other people see and uphold this person as a hero. This is exactly what happens to Steve Rogers in the movie. Dr. Erskine sees and affirms that this weakling of a man has the character and moral fiber to be Captain America.

To be set apart and chosen is to be anointed. The word *anoint* means "to apply oil to a person or thing." In the Bible, the word *anoint* is connected to religious ceremonies, for example, as a way to set apart a place (Genesis 28:18), ceremonial furnishings (Exodus 40:9–10), priestly garments (Leviticus 8:30), religious leaders (Exodus 28:41), and kings (1 Kings 1:39). When a person is anointed by God's command, it shows that God has conferred holiness and authority on that person.

Maybe the most memorable anointing in the Old Testament was the one performed by the prophet Samuel. King Saul had become disobedient to the will of God and had lost His divine favor. God tasked Samuel with anointing the next king of Israel (even though Saul was still the king, which would prove to be a problem later in the story). The Lord instructed Samuel to fill his horn with oil for the anointing and go to Jesse of Bethlehem. The Lord had determined that the next king of Israel would arise from the house of Jesse.

So Samuel went, and the parade of sons began. First to be considered was Eliab, who was tall and strong—but he's not the guy. Then followed Abinadab, Shammah, and four more brothers to no avail!

> Then Samuel said to Jesse, "Are all your sons here?" And he said, "There remains yet the youngest, but behold, he is keeping the sheep." And Samuel said to Jesse, "Send and get him, for we will not sit down till he comes here." And he sent and brought him in. Now he was ruddy and had beautiful eyes and was handsome. And the LORD said, "Arise, anoint him, for this is he." Then Samuel took the horn of oil and anointed him in the midst of his brothers. And the Spirit of the LORD rushed upon David from that day forward. And Samuel rose up and went to Ramah. (1 SAMUEL 16:11–13)

Okay, so David was a good-looking young man, but he was the youngest of eight brothers and was a shepherd boy. He was not what we would consider a prototype for heroes! How in the world was he going to be the next king? But that is the point! It is not by the world's standards that David was to be king. It was by God's choosing and anointing. God would provide this shepherd boy all he needed to be the next king of Israel. And what was that provision? The Bible simply states, "And the Spirit of the LORD rushed upon David from that day forward" (1 Samuel 16:13).

David received the Spirit of the Lord. Steve Rogers would receive microinjections to turn him into Captain America. Anointed by Samuel or anointed by Dr. Erskine, and there you have it! Heroes are anointed. And we love our heroes. But where does that leave you and me? Where does that leave the person traversing the ways of this life who will never reach the stature of a hero by worldly standards? What if I told you that you, too, can be like David?

What if I told you that many of the qualities that we admire in Captain America are offered to you out of the hand of the Lord?

In the darkness of night, a Pharisee and ruler of the Jewish people came to Jesus. His name was Nicodemus. Nicodemus was in search of more—spiritual insight, closeness with God, and abiding peace with His creator. When he came to Jesus for spiritual direction, what did he get? "Jesus answered him, 'Truly, truly, I say to you, unless one is born again he cannot see the kingdom of God'" (John 3:3). Born again? Nicodemus scoffs at the notion of entering into his mother's womb a second time and starting life over! But Jesus elaborates: "Truly, truly, I say to you, unless one is born of water and the Spirit, he cannot enter the kingdom of God" (John 3:5).

Water and the Spirit. Born again. Baptism. The anointing we need is found in Baptism. Martin Luther explains the clear benefits of Baptism this way: "It works forgiveness of sins, rescues from death and devil, and gives eternal salvation to all who believe this, as the words and promises of God declare."[28] Okay, so Baptism doesn't make us a superhero like Steve Rogers or a biblical icon like David. And it is way more than our working definition of anointing!

Baptism is sacramental. The Lutheran Church understands Baptism as a sacred act "instituted by the command of Christ," an act "in which Christ joins His Word of promise to a visible element . . . [and] by which He offers and bestows the forgiveness of sins He has earned for us by His suffering, death, and resurrection."[29] The old Adam is drowned and the new man arises. No spiritual ninety-eight-pound weakling here! Through the waters of Baptism,

28 Small Catechism, Baptism, Second Part; *Luther's Small Catechism with Explanation* (St. Louis: Concordia Publishing House, 2017), 23.

29 Small Catechism, 282 (Question 293).

you are a transformed child of God. So don't be a superhero. Be a washed and cleansed child of God!

BRAVE

A hero is the embodiment of the word *brave*. A hero is extraordinary because a hero stands when others fall. A hero rushes into a burning building to save others while the masses run from the flames. A hero sees the suffering of others and moves to action while the majority runs from danger. A hero puts others before his or her own safety while the crowds seek protection for themselves. Because heroes are brave, they live their lives engaging in acts of bravery. Bravery is the demonstration of courage in the face of personal peril. In other words, the hero is willing to risk all for the benefit, care, and protection of other people, regardless of whether those people are deserving.

Steve Rogers—Captain America—is the epitome of brave. When confronted with the prospect of his friend Bucky and the men of the 107th Infantry Regiment being captured thirty miles behind enemy lines, Captain America has but one action to take: rescue these men. Armed with only a shield and a handgun, he jumps out of an airplane behind enemy lines, an army of one going up against the dreaded Red Skull and his Hydra troops with their futuristic weapons. Miraculously, he frees the prisoners and rescues Bucky, coming face-to-face with Red Skull himself! He is not deterred by this enemy and rescues the captured soldiers through his inspirational actions and leadership. And how does he finish this all off? By leading the rescued soldiers thirty miles across enemy territory, back to the American camp where this all began.[30]

30 To view these scenes, watch from 51:58 to 1:12:02 (scenes 8–10).

Heroes are willing to walk into overwhelming danger. Heroes are willing to encounter overwhelming odds because that is exactly what the world needs them to do. Captain America goes because he is needed, demonstrating his bravery in the face of adversity. The newly anointed future king of Israel was also brave. Shortly after David's anointing, the Israelite army was at a standstill with the Philistines. The Philistines boasted of a champion named Goliath—giant in stature and ego. He struck fear in the hearts of the Israelites, including King Saul. Who would have guessed that a young shepherd boy would be willing to stand against overwhelming odds for the sake of a people cowering in the presence of the Philistines and their giant?

But that is exactly what David did. David was inspirational and articulate: "Who is this uncircumcised Philistine, that he should defy the armies of the living God?" (1 Samuel 17:26). David showed no fear. Where his fellow countrymen saw a giant, David saw only an uncircumcised Philistine who had the audacity to stand in the face of the armies of the living God! Even when King Saul offered him armor and a helmet to wear to this uneven match, David refused, taking only a staff, a sling, and five smooth stones. What unfolded is the stuff that defines the bravery of a hero!

> The Philistine said to David, "Come to me, and I will give your flesh to the birds of the air and to the beasts of the field." Then David said to the Philistine, "You come to me with a sword and with a spear and with a javelin, but I come to you in the name of the LORD of hosts, the God of the armies of Israel, whom you have defied. This day the LORD will deliver you into my hand, and I will strike you down and cut off your head. And I will give the dead bodies of the host of

> the Philistines this day to the birds of the air and to the wild beasts of the earth, that all the earth may know that there is a God in Israel, and that all this assembly may know that the LORD saves not with sword and spear. For the battle is the LORD's, and He will give you into our hand."
>
> When the Philistine arose and came and drew near to meet David, David ran quickly toward the battle line to meet the Philistine. And David put his hand in his bag and took out a stone and slung it and struck the Philistine on his forehead. The stone sank into his forehead, and he fell on his face to the ground.
>
> So David prevailed over the Philistine with a sling and with a stone, and struck the Philistine and killed him. There was no sword in the hand of David. (1 SAMUEL 17:44–50)

A slingshot and a stone. All the bravado and size of the Philistine giant could not deter David. David did not cower in fear of this giant but ran toward him when the battle began! David possessed confidence that flowed from his faith in God, the God who chose him out of all of his brothers and all of Israel, the God who had Samuel anoint him with oil. Now, with a steady hand and cool demeanor, David did what heroes do: he was brave in the face of danger for the sake of his people.

However, bravery is not found only in those who stand before giants or supervillains on the big screen. A simple confession of faith and sharing of the Gospel can be considered brave. Take the apostle Paul. He wrote to the Church in Thessalonica: "But though we had already suffered and been shamefully treated at Philippi, as you know, we had boldness in our God to declare to you the gospel of God in the midst of much conflict" (1 Thessalonians 2:2).

Paul's strength and bravery flowed from his conviction of faith in Jesus Christ. Paul saw those who were hostile to the Gospel just as David saw Goliath!

The saving grace of Jesus Christ provides the believer with confidence and certainty. The apostle Paul uses the word *power* to describe the Gospel. Paul states, "For I am not ashamed of the gospel, for it is the power of God for salvation to everyone who believes, to the Jew first and also to the Greek" (Romans 1:16). This power of God is distinctive from the power of humans. Martin Luther explains the difference between the two like this:

> [The power of humans] is the power by which man gains strength and health according to the flesh and by which he is able to do the things which are of the flesh. But this power God completely canceled by the cross of Christ in order to give His own power, by which the spirit becomes strong and is saved and by which one is able to do the things of the spirit, Psalm 60:11–12: "Vain is the help of man. With God we shall do valiantly."[31]

By grace through faith in Jesus Christ, you have received such power from God. This gift of God gives you confidence and peace. This gift allows you to remain firm even when persecution and hardship befall you. Maybe you do not see yourself as brave when you measure your life against the likes of Captain America (who is a fictional superhero, after all!) or even a biblical superstar like David. But here's the good news: Don't be a hero! Instead, be filled with the power of God for your salvation. Why? Because that is what you really need.

---

31 Martin Luther, Luther's Works, vol. 25 (St. Louis: Concordia Publishing House, 1972), 149–50.

SACRIFICIAL

A hero is willing to go to extraordinary lengths to rescue and save others. The hero is willing to put his life on the line so that others may live and be free. In an intense and climactic moment, Steve Rogers has gone after Red Skull to foil his plot to destroy major cities in the United States. Red Skull must be stopped, and Captain America is the only man for the job. After all, he's the hero of the movie! Captain America launches himself onto an airplane that is loaded with bombs bound for the United States.

After high-stakes drama and fighting, the Hydra soldiers are vanquished, leaving only Captain America and Red Skull on the plane. The battle ensues. Good versus evil. Only one can win. And just like that, Red Skull is destroyed—and we so wish this were the conclusion of the movie! But it's not. Captain America is left alone on the plane loaded with explosives bound for the United States. Then Captain America does what heroes do: he sacrifices himself by crashing the plane into the frozen waters of the Arctic Ocean. He sacrifices himself for the sake of humanity. Captain America is a hero.[32]

Throughout the Bible, many key people emerge victorious when defending the people of God. Their lives end peacefully after years of leading and defending the people of God. Other men and women in the pages of Scripture suffer for their faith and their people. Scripture is filled with people who lived, led, and died. But they were not brought to the point of sacrificing themselves for the sake of those they served.

---

32 To view these scenes, watch from 1:33:54 to 1:48:45 (scenes 14–15).

Jesus is one exception to this scriptural truth. Jesus stands apart from the rest of the cast of characters found in the pages of the Bible. His birth was prophesied, and His arrival was anticipated. He was born of a virgin and raised in a dusty, inconsequential village. When He burst onto the scene, He was identified by the voice of the Father and overshadowed by the lighting of the Holy Spirit. He performed miracles, walked on water, fed large crowds, and cast out demons. He taught with authority and challenged the religious elite. He was endeared to people because of His love, compassion, and mercy.

But Jesus is so much more than all of that. As we say in the Second Article of the Apostles' Creed:

> I believe . . . in Jesus Christ, His only Son, our Lord, who was conceived by the Holy Spirit, born of the Virgin Mary, suffered under Pontius Pilate, was crucified, died and was buried. He descended into hell. The third day He rose again from the dead. He ascended into heaven and sits at the right hand of God, the Father Almighty. From thence He will come to judge the living and the dead.[33]

The Second Article of the Creed spends the majority of its confessional space on Jesus' once-for-all sacrifice for the forgiveness of sins. Look how Martin Luther explains this:

> [Jesus] has redeemed me, a lost and condemned person, purchased and won me from all sins, from death, and from the power of the devil; not with gold or silver, but with His holy, precious blood and with His innocent suffering and death, that I may be His own and live under Him in His

33 Small Catechism, Second Article; *Luther's Small Catechism with Explanation*, 17.

> kingdom and serve Him in everlasting righteousness, innocence, and blessedness, just as He is risen from the dead, lives and reigns to all eternity. This is most certainly true.[34]

Jesus is so much more than a hero. Jesus is the King of kings and Lord of lords. He alone defeats sin, death, and the devil on behalf of sinful people. What Jesus does for us is more than heroic. It is salvific! As the apostle Paul writes:

> For while we were still weak, at the right time Christ died for the ungodly. For one will scarcely die for a righteous person—though perhaps for a good person one would dare even to die—but God shows His love for us in that while we were still sinners, Christ died for us. Since, therefore, we have now been justified by His blood, much more shall we be saved by Him from the wrath of God. For if while we were enemies we were reconciled to God by the death of His Son, much more, now that we are reconciled, shall we be saved by His life. More than that, we also rejoice in God through our Lord Jesus Christ, through whom we have now received reconciliation. (ROMANS 5:6–11)

What Jesus Christ does for us is born out of love and is alien to our experience. His sacrifice reconciles us to the Father. "'Reconciliation' describes God's act on the Cross in personal terms, just as 'justification' describes it in terms of law and justice. One act of God is thus described from two points of view, both valid, both necessary. . . . Christ's death has reconciled us to God; He

---

34 Small Catechism, Second Article; *Luther's Small Catechism with Explanation*, 17.

rose from that death to be our living Lord, at the right hand of God, interceding for us."[35]

Jesus did that for the whole world. Jesus is the one and only Savior who can reconcile the world to the heavenly Father. He alone is the grand exclamation point for a fallen and broken world. Even Hollywood wants to capture the power of a resurrected hero. Steve Rogers goes down with the plane, sinking into an icy tomb in the Arctic Ocean. Alas, the hero has died saving his people—or has he? The movie ends with Captain America waking up in a hospital. By all appearances, it is 1945. But something is amiss, and Steve Rogers knows it. Running from the hospital room, he emerges into Times Square in New York. The problem? It is seventy years later! It appears our hero somehow survived a seventy-year hibernation in the frozen waters of the Arctic.[36]

The Gospel story of Jesus is powerful and transformative. It's no wonder that Hollywood is captivated by a story of life and death and life again. But all Captain America can do is be Captain America. All he can do is be brave, defend the weak, stand up for the little guy, and protect the innocent. Even seventy years later, he is still Steve Rogers—a man anointed with superhuman strength. Jesus is so much more. He was anointed in the Jordan River, walked bravely and steadfastly to the cross, sacrificed Himself for the sins of the world, and rose victoriously on the third day. This is heroic to the core. And therein lies the truth for you and me: we don't have to be heroes because we are followers of Jesus, the true hero. So don't be a hero! Instead, be a child of God!

---

35 Martin Franzmann, *Romans: A Commentary* (St. Louis: Concordia Publishing House, 1968), commentary on 5:10.

36 To view this scene, watch from 1:50:45 to 1:53:50 (scene 16).

Discussion Questions

1. Define the word *hero*. Create a list of people (either real or fictional) whom you have considered heroes. What qualities and attributes do these people share? What are their differences?

2. Make a list of figures from the Bible who are considered heroic. What makes them heroic? What are their shortcomings? How does God work in and through their lives for the sake of others?

3. What does the word *anoint* mean? Read 1 Samuel 16:12; 2 Kings 9:3. What did anointing signify in the Old Testament? How is Baptism related to anointing?

4. In the movie *Captain America: The First Avenger*, Steve Rogers demonstrates extraordinary bravery. What is bravery? Whom do you consider brave today?

5. Read 1 Samuel 17. What verses speak to the bravery of David? What verses speak to the weakness and fears of his brothers and fellow Israelites?

6. Read Romans 1 and 1 Thessalonians 2. What is the "power of God" (Romans 1:16)? How does that power strengthen you in the face of adversity?

7. Captain America appears to die a sacrificial death. Whom does it benefit? Jesus Christ dies a sacrificial death on the cross. How do you receive the gift Jesus gives through His death and resurrection? How is Jesus more than a hero? Who is Jesus for you?

8. What challenged you in this scene? What did you find affirming to your faith?

TICKET
THE END
CINEMA
MOVIE
TICKET
THE END

SCENE 5

ORDINARY IS EXTRAORDINARY

FEATURE PRESENTATION

JUDY

A mother and father innocently ask their little child: "What do you want to be when you grow up?" After a moment of thoughtful consideration, the child may answer with careers such as movie star, baseball player, dancer, or artist. And so it begins: the pursuit of the extraordinary. The notion that my child is meant for more, will be more, will accomplish more than other children ricochets between the ears of the mother and father. "My child is the smartest in her preschool class." "My daughter has been recommended for advanced dance lessons." "My son throws the baseball harder than any other kid out there." The pursuit of the extraordinary begins with thoughts like these.

In many respects, it is a parental trap. On one hand, parents want to encourage their child to dream big and pursue life with vigor; on the other hand, the child's dreams may be grander than his or her abilities (or a parent's financial capacity). But parents are willing to do just about anything so their child can stretch to the lofty heights of the extraordinary. Little League fields, dance studios, ice-skating rinks, golf courses, and basketball courts are littered with the hopes and dreams of parents seeking the extraordinary from and for their child. Sacrifices are made and dreams are nurtured, all in the hopes of arriving at the extraordinary.

And why not? Who doesn't want their child to succeed, to be successful, to be extraordinary? Oh, how pride comes creeping in around the edges. Who doesn't like to boast of their child's accomplishments and achievements? How quick we are to show off our children's skills and quietly pat ourselves on the back for a job well done. In this digitally driven age, with a simple tap or keystroke, our entire parental and familial networks are notified of the latest and greatest success of our children. "Look at what my son has done!" "See how great my daughter is doing!" "My child is *extraordinary*!"

But wait a minute! It's not only parents who push children down the pathway toward extraordinary! Children are quite capable of being bit by the extraordinary bug as well. The boy runs down the field as the football gently drops into his hands. The girl steps on the soccer field and dreams of playing for Team USA. The child sits behind his or her keyboard, thinking about the creation of the next great video game. The student pores over the pages of history and science books, considering how to reach for the stars and be the first person to step on Mars.

Children don't necessarily need their parents' push to dream (and believe) that they will be extraordinary. Influences such as school, the internet, and entertainment are powerful draws for children to think that everything is within their grasp. After all, what pushed you? What prodded you to strive, reach, and stretch for your extraordinary? But children also have to live with disappointment when they don't achieve the extraordinary and fall short of their dreams. The weight can be heavy. Society says, "Dream big," but it fails to catch you when you fall short of the glory.

WHAT HAPPENED TO "ORDINARY"?

Whatever happened to the days when a child dreamed of being a firefighter, a police officer, a teacher, or an electrician? Where have the days gone when it was noble to be a carpenter, a plumber, a pastor, or an engineer? In other words, what happened to ordinary? Now, don't get me wrong—these jobs (along with a host of many others) are incredibly important; they take dedication, skill, and intelligence; they are necessary for the good of society. But they aren't flashy by the standards of a digitally driven age. They don't command high dollars in wages (which is the measuring stick of our Western capitalist society). And they won't get your image plastered anywhere and everywhere (the benchmark of the digitally savvy community). Ordinary is simply not good enough. We crave more!

However, the overwhelming majority of people in the world live and labor in the ordinary. Ordinary people living ordinary lives. They rise in the morning and drive their family sedan to work, work long hours, have too little time for their family, and yearn for a vacation. They will never amass millions of dollars. They will never exceed the friends limit on Facebook or some other social-media platform. And outside of their close-knit network of family and friends, when they die, the remainder of society will not remember them. They will live, labor, love, and die in the embrace of the ordinary.

By no means is this a new phenomenon or recent societal trend. The ordinary has been with us forever. Glance through the pages of a history book, and what do you see? A handful of extraordinary people surrounded by ordinary, everyday folk.

Take President Ronald Reagan. There he stood in front of the Berlin Wall, delivering one of the most memorable speeches of the twentieth century. But on that day, he was not alone. He was surrounded by tens of thousands of ordinary people seeking a free and united Germany—people whose names were never recorded but without whose presence the speech would never have been delivered.

What about the world of music? The rock singer Bono has influenced the world with his music through the band U2, and he has made an enormous social impact through humanitarian work, such as Live Aid. But he hasn't done it alone. On July 13, 1985, some 72,000 ordinary people packed a stadium in London while another 89,484 people packed a stadium in Philadelphia to see U2 and many other musicians perform for the Live Aid concert, all to raise money for and bring awareness of world hunger. Ordinary people participated in a global movement to end world hunger.

And let's not leave out the Church! In eighteenth-century America, Great Awakening preacher George Whitefield traveled over five thousand miles to deliver thunderous sermons. But he didn't do this in empty churches or vacant fields. He preached his sermons to ordinary colonists, slaves, and Native Americans—common people who remain anonymous on the pages of history and institutional memory, standing in the shadow of what the world considers to be extraordinary!

THE BIBLICALLY ORDINARY

If we view Scripture through a worldly lens, we can be drawn to the amazing, spectacular, and faith-filled characters that populate the sacred pages. Names such as Noah and Abraham, Moses and

Joshua, Ruth and Esther, David and Solomon fill our collective imaginations and demonstrate extraordinary faith in life and action. These are the biblical giants! We have heard their stories over and over from Sunday School on. If only I had the faith of fill-in-the-blank, my life would be so much *more*; it would not be so ordinary!

But maybe we need to look deeper. Maybe we need to go beyond the big names of the Bible to find where the ordinary, everyday people dwell—people whose lives are often forgotten or overlooked but who made extraordinary contributions to the story of salvation. These ordinary people had a profound impact on our story of life and faith. After all, they worked and served in faithfulness, labored and traveled in devotion so that the story of the Extraordinary of extraordinaries, Jesus Christ, would be made known to the world.

Who are the ordinary, overlooked, and rarely mentioned people of the Bible that I am talking about? Many examples are scattered across the pages of Scripture, but let's consider just a few. In the Book of Exodus, we read about two men by the names of Bezalel (the son of Uri, son of Hur, of the tribe of Judah) and Oholiab (the son of Ahisamach, of the tribe of Dan). Haven't heard of them? You should have! They arrived on the scene in Exodus 31 and were indispensable in the construction of the tabernacle, the ark of the covenant, the table, the lampstand, the altar of incense, the altar of burnt offering, the bronze basin, and the court.[37] These master craftsmen, filled with the Spirit of God, contributed their work to the building of the ark of the covenant and all of the surrounding furnishings! The ordinary contributed to the extraordinary!

---

37 For a complete review of Bezalel's and Oholiab's contributions, read Exodus 35:30–38:20.

Just as Bezalel and Oholiab crafted a physical house for the Lord, the ordinary couple Aquila and Priscilla were busy building a spiritual house for the fledgling Church of the Way. Aquila was a tentmaker, a Christian Jew who was expelled from Rome for causing quarrels in the synagogues of the city. Now he and his wife were living in Corinth. It was here in Corinth that they would become co-workers in Gospel ministry with Paul (see Acts 18:1–3). But this couple desired to serve the Lord wherever He led. From Corinth, they journeyed with Paul to Ephesus (see Acts 18:18–21). They remained in Ephesus to nurture the fledgling Christian community and establish a church in their home.[38] These ordinary missionaries are mentioned here and there in the New Testament, and Paul clearly appreciated their labor and love for the Lord because he mentioned them several times in his epistles—an ordinary couple making an extraordinary impact in ministry.

Ordinary people accomplishing extraordinary things in the name of the Lord. It is relevant, relatable, and biblical. God chooses and uses people in all of their ordinariness to accomplish and achieve great things for His name's sake. But what happens to the quest for the extraordinary life? Is it abandoned? Is it chasing after fool's gold? Is it ultimately seeking self-glory at the expense of an emotionally and spiritually healthy life?

---

38 For further reading on Aquila and Priscilla, see 1 Corinthians 16:19; 2 Timothy 4:19; Romans 16:4. This missionary couple does not have volumes of Scripture recounting their activity. However, they were clearly important to the missional activity of the apostle Paul and even risked their own lives for his safety (see Romans 16:3–4).

THE EXTRAORDINARY QUEST FOR ORDINARY

The quest for the extraordinary is not all that it is cracked up to be! In fact, the world is littered with the carcasses of broken, beaten, and battered extraordinary people. How often do you find a headline on your newsfeed of an extraordinary and famous person who has prematurely died because of drug abuse, alcohol abuse, or self-inflicted injuries? From musicians to actors, athletes to global leaders, these people stood on the precipice of extraordinary, received all the accolades and praises of an adoring public, and suddenly crashed and burned right before our eyes.

In 2019, director Rupert Goold and BBC Films brought to the big screen the story of beloved actress and singer Judy Garland (played by Renée Zellweger). The movie follows the steps of Garland as she arrives in London in 1968 to perform at a series of sold-out concerts. It is thirty years since Judy Garland rose to stardom for the role of Dorothy in *The Wizard of Oz.* She is loved by adoring fans, is blessed with the voice of an angel, and commands the stage like no other. But that is only what the public sees—an extraordinary talent that soars above the fray. The movie takes the viewer on a journey behind the wizard's curtain of fame and fortune to peer into an extraordinary life that seems to be on a quest for the ordinary.[39]

---

39 *Judy*, directed by Rupert Goold (2019; Santa Monica, CA: Lionsgate Entertainment, 2019), DVD.

"THAT VOICE"

Even if you are not a moviegoer, you have probably run into *The Wizard of Oz* somewhere. The movie was filmed in 1939 in both black-and-white and Technicolor, and it tells the story of young Dorothy (played by Judy Garland) being swept away to the magical land of Oz. Technicolor, music, dance, creative characters, witches, a wizard, a castle, and of course, a yellow brick road to travel down. If you are one of those people who have never seen *The Wizard of Oz*, put down this book immediately! I mean it! Go find a copy and watch it. I promise it will be worth your time, and I will wait.[40]

Welcome back to those of you who had to step out and watch *The Wizard of Oz.* As promised, I waited for you. Now back to our story. The movie *Judy* begins with a seventeen-year-old Judy Garland walking on the set of *The Wizard of Oz* with Louis B. Mayer, the film producer and co-founder of Metro-Goldwyn-Mayer Studios (MGM). Judy Garland had been working for MGM Studios since age 13. Her life is consumed with making movies, and she's tired. She's worn out. Just outside the gates of MGM Studios is an ocean of ordinary that this seventeen-year-old girl longs for—high school, boys, dances, soda shops, cheeseburgers, and anything else a girl growing up in the 1930s would consider a part of her daily life and routine. What those outside of the gates of the movie studio considered ordinary, Judy Garland desired.

---

40 Directed by Victor Fleming, the film was released in 1939. The film was considered a critical success but failed to make the profits MGM Studios hoped for, due to the high budget. The film was rereleased in 1949 and earned only $3,017,000 on a $2,777,000 budget, which did not include the promotional costs. It wasn't until 1956, when the film made its television debut, that it was finally embraced by the public. The film is now considered the most-seen film in movie history.

Mayer confronts Judy Garland about what is beyond the gates—ordinary people who work hard and live off of the dreams that the movies provide. He reminds Judy that in every town there are probably girls who are prettier than her. But what separates Judy from the rest of those pretty girls is "that voice." Judy possesses a voice that can take her places where the pretty girls simply cannot go. Those pretty girls will go on to be cashiers or housewives, and life will be hard on them. Mayer pushes Judy, telling her that her voice will make her a million dollars before she turns twenty, and he gives her a challenge: she can go out there, and the ordinary world will swallow her up and she will be forgotten, or she can stay with the studio and be extraordinary. What seventeen-year-old girl wouldn't choose extraordinary? What seventeen-year-old girl would shun the possibility of being the star?[41]

Physical beauty, athletic skill, artistic talent, and intellectual prowess can be powerful intoxicants for many people. When others recognize any of these characteristics in an individual, that person is often set apart, placed on a pedestal, or simply viewed differently from the rest. Those people possess something that others value. They are differentiated from the mass of society. They are extraordinary.

For most of us, it is hard to relate to Judy Garland's dilemma. I am sure many of those who read these words love to sing. But most of us have never commanded the world's stage with their voice quite like Judy Garland. As much as I love to play golf (and I am sure there are those of you reading who enjoy participating in a variety of sports), I will never be able to do with a golf club what people like Tiger Woods or Phil Mickelson have accomplished

41 To view this scene, watch from 1:12 to 5:22 (scene 1, "Dreams").

playing the same game. The point is simple: there are extraordinary people who work incredibly hard using their God-given abilities and talents. And no matter how hard the rest of us work, study, or practice, we will never quite reach the stratosphere of excellence in which these extraordinary people dwell.

So what do we do when we encounter these extraordinary people? Either we enjoy and celebrate their greatness, or we become resentful that it is them and not us. Simply ignoring the extraordinary is a near-impossible task! The media that bombards us daily will not let us have no opinion. We are pushed and prodded to react. But this isn't just a twenty-first-century conundrum—far from it! In the Bible, Joseph was a young boy in the complicated family tree of Jacob. Jacob had twelve sons by two wives (who were also sisters) and two concubines. Not the most functional family tree you will find in the Bible! Joseph was the eleventh of the twelve sons of Jacob, born to Rachel, the wife Jacob loved. The Bible also tells us that Jacob "loved Joseph more than any other of his sons, because he was the son of his old age. And he made him a robe of many colors" (Genesis 37:3). Not only was Joseph the favorite, but he also received special gifts and treatment from dear old Dad. Not exactly a recipe for a peaceful home life. No wonder Joseph's brothers were angry and jealous!

However, Joseph was also an extraordinary young man. He had vivid dreams with deep meanings and was given the gift of interpreting those dreams. Unfortunately, one of those dreams pictured his brothers bowing down before him. That wasn't well received. "His brothers said to him, 'Are you indeed to reign over us? Or are you indeed to rule over us?' So they hated him even more for his dreams and for his words" (Genesis 37:8). Either we put extraordinary people on a pedestal, or we strive to knock them down. Our discomfort with the extraordinary is born from our struggle with the ordinariness of our own lives. I cannot sing like Judy Garland, I cannot play golf like Tiger Woods or Phil Mickelson, and I cannot interpret dreams like Joseph. So what am I? I am ordinary, and that's okay.

THE STRUGGLE OF EXTRAORDINARY

As we look at the lives of truly extraordinary people, they are not always what they seem. Sure, we see the money and fame, the jewelry and clothing, the lifestyle and the spotlight, the friends and the entourage, and the homes in which they live. But when the ordinary public gets to look behind the wizard's curtain, what they see doesn't always add up to the mental picture they have created regarding the extraordinary. What the ordinary discover is that the extraordinary have struggles, problems, and trials just like the rest of us. Often, those problems are extraordinary as well, equal to the fame and success of their extraordinary lives.

In the movie *Judy*, we discover such a state of affairs. Judy Garland is out of money. In fact, her situation is so desperate that she is homeless. Her ex-husband has temporary custody of their two children. She doesn't even have the resources to get a manager to take control of her failing career. She is left with only one option, and it's one she really doesn't want to pursue: go to London, England, and perform there for three months over the Christmas holiday. Her dilemma is that the court would never let her take her children with her. At this moment in her life, all she wants is to be with her children and be their mother. But her extraordinary life is falling apart before our eyes. Judy Garland is broken and cannot find an answer to her personal chaos. The answer isn't somewhere over the rainbow. Maybe the answer is across the pond in England.[42]

Extraordinary people sometimes have extraordinary problems. And their problems are not usually hidden behind closed doors. In today's social-media-driven, twenty-four-hour-news-cycle, internet-invasive world, their problems are on full display all the time. All I have to do is pick up my phone, and I have an immediate window into their chaos. But imagine if your problems were recorded in the pages of Scripture to be read and studied by generations. Your problems would be on view forever!

This brings us back to Joseph. Even though he was an extraordinary person, he had extraordinary problems to match his stature. One day, Jacob sent Joseph out to check on his brothers. When he was still a ways off, his brothers quipped: "Here comes this dreamer. Come now, let us kill him and throw him into one of the pits. Then we will say that a fierce animal has devoured him, and we will see what will become of his dreams" (Genesis 37:19–20). Ah, "this dreamer"—dripping with sarcasm, I'm sure.

Jealousy, rage, and maybe even a little self-loathing consumed the brothers—except for Reuben. Reuben, the eldest brother, interceded on Joseph's behalf so that the other brothers wouldn't kill him. However, his intercession did not prevent the brothers from selling Joseph into slavery for twenty shekels of silver to the Ishmaelites. And just like that, the extraordinary dreamer and interpreter of dreams was gone. Joseph's problems had just begun!

Joseph arrived in Egypt and was sold to Potiphar, an officer of Pharaoh and captain of the guard. Life began to look up a little. He used his talents and abilities to rise in Potiphar's eyes, eventually

---

42 To view this scene, watch from 21:23 to 28:03 (scene 4, "Children").

becoming the overseer of the house. That is, of course, until Potiphar's wife entered the picture. "Now Joseph was handsome in form and appearance. And after a time his master's wife cast her eyes on Joseph and said, 'Lie with me'" (Genesis 39:6–7). You and I know this would not end well for Joseph! Like the romantic entanglements of an afternoon soap opera, Potiphar's wife was persistent!

> But one day, when he went into the house to do his work and none of the men of the house was there in the house, she caught him by his garment, saying, "Lie with me." But he left his garment in her hand and fled and got out of the house. And as soon as she saw that he had left his garment in her hand and had fled out of the house, she called to the men of her household and said to them, "See, he has brought among us a Hebrew to laugh at us. He came in to me to lie with me, and I cried out with a loud voice. And as soon as he heard that I lifted up my voice and cried out, he left his garment beside me and fled and got out of the house." Then she laid up his garment by her until his master came home, and she told him the same story, saying, "The Hebrew servant, whom you have brought among us, came in to me to laugh at me. But as soon as I lifted up my voice and cried, he left his garment beside me and fled out of the house."
>
> As soon as his master heard the words that his wife spoke to him, "This is the way your servant treated me," his anger was kindled. And Joseph's master took him and put him into the prison, the place where the king's prisoners were confined, and he was there in prison. (GENESIS 37:11–20)

Because of his stunning good looks, Joseph was now in jail—because his master's wife couldn't keep her hands off of him and he refused her advances! I have to admit, I have never, ever had this problem. My ordinary looks might have something to do with that. I don't travel in circles in which I am necessarily exposed to people whose morals might be considered loose or unbounded. What I do know is that ordinary, everyday people also face challenges and conundrums that cause us to struggle like Judy Garland and Joseph. Marital infidelity, divorce, financial upheaval, job loss, addictions, and troubles with the law can nip at our heels. The only difference? Our struggles and chaos probably won't make the evening news or a social-media feed. Instead, we circle the wagons and shut out as much of the world as possible. Why? Because, just like the extraordinary people do, we want our struggles to go away. We want peace in our land. It's not only the extraordinary who struggle. We do too!

WHEN ORDINARY AND EXTRAORDINARY INTERSECT

The ordinary and the extraordinary do not live in isolation from each other. There are many instances in which the two societal worlds are in close proximity. The extraordinary is on the stage, playing field, or arena while surrounded by the myriad of ordinary people. We watch while they perform. But in rare moments, the two worlds intersect—when the extraordinary and the ordinary find themselves face-to-face in conversation, piercing the barrier between each other's lives. These moments can be exhilarating, inspiring, and memorable.

I can still remember June 16, 2006, with profound clarity. I had taken my son to the US Open Golf Tournament at Winged Foot Golf Club in Mamaroneck, New York. At the time, my son was all of nine years old. As we sat on the fifteenth tee box, there was a backup in play due to a golfer losing his ball down the fairway. While sitting there, my son's favorite golfer came walking up to the tee box: Phil Mickelson. My son loved Phil because, like Phil, he plays golf left-handed (a rarity in the golfing world, and I should know—I'm left-handed too!). But Phil didn't stand off to the side of the tee box with his caddy, Jim "Bones" Mackay. No, the extraordinary, Phil Mickelson, chose to intersect with the ordinary, my son. Phil walked over and squatted down to my son's height. He started a conversation: Who is your favorite golfer? Do you play golf left- or right-handed? Are you having a good time? All this during a major golf championship! And then Phil reached into his pocket and handed my son a golf ball (which he still has to this day). Worlds collided, and the ordinary felt extraordinary because of the extraordinary doing the most ordinary of things—sharing a simple conversation with a child.

The movie *Judy* includes a similar scene in which worlds intersect, where the extraordinary and the ordinary share a genuine moment. Following one of her performances in London, Judy Garland exits the theater late at night. Standing outside of the theater are two men—groupies, if you will—waiting to get her autograph and shower her with praise and adoration. In this moment, worlds will collide; the extraordinary and the ordinary are about to break through the barrier between them.

The ensuing conversation outside the back door of the theater is at first what you would expect: awkward and starstruck. The two men share: "We have seen you perform every night this week."

"Your music bypasses the ears and goes straight to the heart." And then the collision: Judy asks these two ordinary fans to enter her world and have dinner with her. There is just one small problem. Nothing is open after midnight on a Tuesday in 1960s London. In a demure and humble tone, the men invite Judy Garland to their apartment, where they can make her an omelet, and she accepts. As the evening unfolds, Judy ends up doing the cooking. They play cards and share life stories, and she even sings while one man plays the piano. In that moment, Judy shares a simple but powerful sentiment: she tells them that it is sweet that they come to see her every night and that it makes her feel like she has allies. The extraordinary is served by the ordinary, and the ordinary in this moment has become extraordinary to her.[43]

Let's revisit Joseph, the extraordinary biblical personality. After the incident with Potiphar's wife, he was in prison (Genesis 39). But the Lord was with him, and he found favor in the eyes of the keeper of the prison—so much so that he put Joseph in charge of the prisoners! If this doesn't reinforce in your mind how extraordinary Joseph was, I'm not sure anything will. While Joseph kept things peaceful among the prisoners, two new inmates entered the picture: the cupbearer and baker for the Pharaoh. They had caused some offense to the Pharaoh, and as a result, they were imprisoned with Joseph, who was appointed to attend to them.

These two men were in prison for some time. The Bible tells us that "one night they both dreamed . . . each his own dream, and each dream with its own interpretation" (Genesis 40:5). Then came the moment when the extraordinary and the ordinary would intersect. The two men were deeply troubled by their dreams.

43 To view this scene, watch from 50:26 to 57:16 (scene 8, "Dinner?").

So Joseph reached out to them: "'Why are your faces downcast today?' They said to him, 'We have had dreams, and there is no one to interpret them.' And Joseph said to them, 'Do not interpretations belong to God? Please tell them to me'" (Genesis 40:7–8).

What makes Joseph so extraordinary? Joseph himself gave us the answer: he was a servant of God. The servant of God used his extraordinary gifts for the benefit and blessing of others. Joseph used his ability to interpret dreams for the sake of the house of Israel. Maybe his brothers couldn't see that when he shared with them the dream that they would all bow down to him. Maybe the baker didn't like the interpretation of his dream, which revealed that he would be hanged in three days. (I'm not sure any of us would have liked that!) Even the cupbearer couldn't comprehend how significant this collision with Joseph really was—after all, Genesis 40:23–41:1 tells us that he forgot Joseph for two years after that.

But when the time was right, when the Pharaoh was riddled with a dream that he could not understand, the ordinary cupbearer remembered the extraordinary interpreter of dreams and their intersection in the prison. The cupbearer recounted to Pharaoh: "A young Hebrew was there with us, a servant of the captain of the guard. When we told him, he interpreted our dreams to us, giving an interpretation to each man according to his dream. And as he interpreted to us, so it came about. I was restored to my office and the baker was hanged" (Genesis 41:12–13). Despite his forgetfulness, the cupbearer recounted his encounter with the extraordinary young Hebrew, Joseph. That one moment of the ordinary meeting the extraordinary was about to change the fate of Pharaoh, Egypt, Joseph, and the children of Israel!

These intersections show us that the extraordinary and the ordinary are really not that different. People desire relationships and community with other people. Pull back the layers of talent, skill, and giftedness of the extraordinary, and you are left with an ordinary person searching for community and companionship with other ordinary people on life's journey. Through simple conversations, acts of kindness, and demonstrations of love, the walls between extraordinary and ordinary people fall away. Joseph served the baker, cupbearer, Pharaoh, and eventually his own brothers. Judy served two Englishmen and called them allies. Phil Mickelson served my son and provided him with a memory that lasts to this very day. The extraordinary and ordinary intersect with each other, and at those meeting points, both discover how similar they really are.

THE ORDINARY IS EXTRAORDINARY

At these intersections between the ordinary and the extraordinary, we begin to understand that ordinary *is* extraordinary! The ordinary is capable of making a memorable and lasting impact on other people, including the extraordinary! In the closing scene of the movie *Judy*, the extraordinary actress and singer is horribly broken. She has been fired from the show in London. Her life has spiraled out of control. She goes to the theater and asks the replacement performer if she could give the audience one more song. Of course, he gives way to Judy Garland. Who wouldn't yield the stage to this extraordinary talent? And perform she does, belting out a song that brings the audience to their feet with thunderous applause. It is a moment of redemption for her extraordinary talent and faltering career.

And then Judy Garland does the unexpected. She asks permission from the band and the audience to sing one more song. She explains that the song she will sing is not about getting anywhere. Rather, it is a song about "walking toward somewhere that you've dreamed of. And maybe, maybe the walk is every day of your life. And the walking has to be enough. It's about hope, and we all need that." The song? You guessed it: "Over the Rainbow."[44] But as she sings, her heart grows heavy and her soul weary. The extraordinary is melting before the eyes of the onlooking ordinary. Judy stops singing as she tears up. She has realized that she is without hope.

Then, up in the balcony, an ordinary voice begins to sing. And then another voice joins in. Those two voices? The Englishmen who were Judy's proclaimed allies. No longer simple, ordinary fans, they have become extraordinary allies and friends. Soon the whole theater joins in. Judy Garland is filled with love and hope. The ordinary is indeed extraordinary, and the extraordinary knows it and acknowledges it![45]

The impact of simple words, gestures, and acts by ordinary people should never be overlooked or ignored. When people share community and love, they bless and elevate those around them—whether they are ordinary or extraordinary by societal standards. Throughout this chapter, we have looked at Joseph as an extraordinary servant of the Lord. When he finally met his brothers again—yes, those brothers who sold him into slavery and wanted to kill him—he had extraordinary power. He could have exacted revenge on them. But instead, he received them, cared for them, provided for them, and brought them to Egypt so that they could receive out of the abundance of his hand. And what did Joseph

---

44 "Over the Rainbow" was composed by Harold Arlen with lyrics by E. Y. Harburg for *The Wizard of Oz*. It won the Academy Award for best original song and became Judy Garland's signature song.

45 To view this scene, watch from 1:40:34 to 1:51:21 (scene 15, "One Song").

receive in return? Community, family, and long-lost familial love. Oh, sure, Joseph was testing his brothers. But at the same time, why not have a little brotherly fun at their expense! But I think we can forgive him—after all, they did plan to kill him once upon a time, and they did sell him into slavery.[46]

And therein lies the extraordinary moment of this biblical story. Joseph needed his family and desired to be with his family. He loved his family. What we see as rather mundane and ordinary was the one thing lacking in Joseph's life. As Joseph proclaimed to his brothers, "Do not be distressed or angry with yourselves because you sold me here, for God sent me before you to preserve life" (Genesis 45:5). Joseph saw his entire life as preparation for this very moment—to use his extraordinary gifts for this treasure, the preservation of his family.

Judy Garland desired to be a mother to her children. Joseph desired to be a brother to his siblings. And we are given the opportunity to be sons and daughters of the Lord, united through the waters of Baptism and found together in the arms of the Church. What the world sees as ordinary is, in fact, the most extraordinary thing found in the world: the love of family. So we travel down the yellow brick road of life together. As Judy Garland reminds us in the movie, "Maybe the walk is every day of your life. And the walking has to be enough." For Christians, that pathway will lead us to the waiting and loving arms of Jesus, the place where the ordinary is truly extraordinary!

---

46 The account of Joseph and his brothers is a powerful story of forgiveness and love. Read Genesis 42–47 for the full story. In these chapters, we clearly see how the extraordinary servant Joseph demonstrates humility and love as he cares for his brothers and the remainder of his family who had been lost to him for so long.

Discussion Questions

1. How do you define *ordinary*? How do you define *extraordinary*? What do you consider to be an ordinary job? What are extraordinary jobs?

2. Have you ever been in the presence of someone you consider extraordinary? Who was it? How did it make you feel? How did you react to the person? How did you act around him or her?

3. Whom do you consider to be extraordinary people in the Bible? Why do you view them this way? Whom do you consider to be ordinary people in the Bible? Why do view them this way?

4. Name some ordinary people of the Bible who accomplished extraordinary things. How did those accomplishments further the mission of the Church?

5 Judy Garland was extraordinary due to her voice. Joseph was extraordinary due to his ability to interpret dreams. What makes you extraordinary in the eyes of the Lord?

6. Judy Garland's life was challenged by a myriad of problems. Joseph was sold into slavery by his brothers and later imprisoned because of false accusations by an Egyptian woman. What life challenges are you facing? How are your problems different from the problems of extraordinary people?

7. In the movie, Judy Garland states, "Maybe the walk is every day of your life. And the walking has to be enough." How does our everyday walk as ordinary people find extraordinary meaning? As Christians, where does our yellow brick road lead?

8. What challenged you in this scene? What did you find affirming to your faith?

TICKET
THE END
CINEMA
MOVIE
TICKET
THE END

SCENE 6

MODEL MENTORS

FEATURE PRESENTATION

A STAR IS BORN

Take a moment to reminisce. Close your eyes and focus on moments and places that are important to your life's journey. Seriously, close your eyes and reminisce. Take your time. Now, what images came to your mind's eye? What did you see? Where did your mind take you? Maybe a more important question to ask is this: Whom did you see? Your mind may be filled with beautiful scenes of nature, towering skyscrapers, or rolling hills in the country. But chances are that in those images you also saw people. And not just any people. You saw important people—people who have influenced, blessed, and assisted your walk in this world.

For some of you, the images that came to mind were populated with parents and grandparents, sisters and brothers, aunts and uncles. You have been blessed with a loving family that was there for you every step of the way. These people may have provided you boundaries of discipline, wisdom from their experiences, and sound reason and advice regarding your future. These people loved you unconditionally. You laughed together, cried together, and celebrated life together. They were there for you no matter the circumstances.

But that's no longer the norm for many people. In fact, married people today have less than an even chance of still being married twenty-five years later.[47] As a consequence, the family unit has been beaten and battered in the midst of the cultural storm. Others of you reading this know that firsthand. Your family may be a little more complicated. Divorce and divisive behaviors may have eroded the foundation of your family relationships. Your circle of people may be smaller, and so you hold close those rare few who have journeyed through life with you every step of the way.

Some of the people who came to mind are still with you—present-tense people who continue to bless you and bring joy to your heart. Others may be gone, those precious relationships cut short by death and disease, leaving you only memories.

But I want you to consider those beyond your familial boundaries. Other people have also been important to your journey, people who have had a direct and profound impact on your life. These are people who influenced the way you think and how you act. They challenged you to dig deeper, think broader, and dream bigger. They saw the best in you and pushed you to realize your potential. In a very real way, these people become a part of who we are, what we think, and why we do what we do. These people are selfless influencers whom we encounter on our journey. They gave freely of themselves, and we gladly received from their hand.

---

47 Sam Roberts, "Majority of Marriages End Before Twenty-Five Years, Census Finds," *New York Times*, September 19, 2007, https://www.nytimes.com/2007/09/19/us/19cnd-census.html.

THEY ARE ALL AROUND US

Who are these people? They are teachers, coaches, pastors, tutors, musicians, and instructors. They are everyday people who are passionate about their occupation, and we are the fortunate ones who had the privilege of learning from them. We encounter them at school, at church, on sports teams, in dance studios and gyms and music halls. In those encounters, a relationship is born. They give, and we receive. They find a way into our hearts, where they will be cherished forever. Often these people don't even realize how important they have become in our lives. They tirelessly and lovingly keep on giving to any and all who will receive their wisdom, knowledge, encouragement, love, and support. Why do they do this? It is who they are and what they do. Giving selflessly to others is what makes them tick.

What do we call these people? Mentors. A mentor is a person who has experience and knowledge and is willing and eager to share that experience and knowledge with someone else. A mentor is not determined by age; rather, a mentor is determined by expertise and a desire to share knowledge with others. Being a mentor is deeply relational and creates a bond with the learner. What a mentor does is best defined as follows:

> Mentoring is a process for the informal transmission of knowledge, social capital, and the psychosocial support perceived by the recipient as relevant to work, career, or professional development; mentoring entails informal communication, usually face-to-face and during a sustained period of time, between a person who is perceived to have greater relevant

> knowledge, wisdom, or experience (the mentor) and a person who is perceived to have less (the protégé).[48]

THE WHO, WHY, AND WHAT

Whether young or old, mentors are people who have made a profound impact on your life. When I close my eyes and think about who have made an impact on my life, two people immediately come into focus: Mary Ann Cochran and Robert Scudieri. Mrs. Cochran was a high school English teacher in my hometown in New Jersey. Pastor Scudieri was the pastor of the church where my family attended. In the scope and sequence of the world, they are regular people who served in normal occupations. Who are your mentors? Who is your Mary Ann Cochran or Robert Scudieri?

Next, think about why you consider those people as your mentors. Chances are they invested time and energy in you. For example, my English teacher spent time with me expanding my creative horizons. She pushed and prodded me because she knew there was more creativity in me than I was letting out. My pastor did likewise. He would talk with me outside of church and youth group. He would stop by the house to visit. He saw within me a servant's heart and a passion for the Gospel of Jesus Christ, and he wanted to unlock that potential for the Church. How about your mentors? What did they see in you? How did they go the extra mile or invest extra time to unlock what otherwise would have remained untapped?

---

48 Barry Bozeman and Mary K. Feeney, "Toward a Useful Theory of Mentoring: A Conceptual Analysis and Critique," *Administration and Society* 39, no. 6 (October 2007): 731, https://doi.org/10.1177/0095399707304119.

Finally, what did your mentors do for you that forever changed the direction of your life? My English teacher was tough; she was creative with her criticism and grading! She knew how to push my overachieving academic buttons and make me work hard for the best results. And my pastor? I suspect he lifted many prayers with my name attached. He also put me in leadership positions in the ministry at the church. He gave me opportunities to succeed and fail so that I would not only learn theological head knowledge but also grow in my spiritual heart for the kingdom of God. What did your mentors do for you? How did they challenge, encourage, and push you to go the extra mile? What creative opportunities did they put in front of you to help you reach your full potential?

THE BIBLICAL MODEL

Recently, I spoke with my childhood pastor about his mentoring role in my life. (Even years later, mentors never stop mentoring!) He was quick to point out the beautiful biblical model presented in the Book of Acts. The Bible is filled with examples of mentoring relationships, but the one that my pastor pointed out to me may be the pinnacle of biblical mentoring. The mentor is introduced in Acts 4:36–37: "Thus Joseph, who was also called by the apostles Barnabas (which means son of encouragement), a Levite, a native of Cyprus, sold a field that belonged to him and brought the money and laid it at the apostles' feet."

There were many Jewish men living in Israel with the name Joseph. In order to differentiate this Joseph from the other Josephs, the disciples gave him a nickname. And what a nickname they chose: *Barnabas*, which means "son of encouragement." Can you think of a better nickname for a mentor than that? When we meet

Joseph—I mean Barnabas—he has sold a field he owned in order to assist in the common distribution for the Christian community. He is an example of Christian charity and love for the Church. But his story was just beginning. Not only was he an encouragement to the disciples, but he would also become the great encourager and mentor for Saul of Tarsus.

Saul was a well-placed Jew who first appears in the Book of Acts as a persecutor of the Early Church. And not just any persecutor. He was a really, really good persecutor, arresting both men and women for following Jesus. Then, on his way to Damascus to persecute more Christians, he had an encounter with Jesus—a powerful encounter that forever changed his life. No longer would Saul be a persecutor of Christians. Instead, he was now a fellow believer.[49] But these evangelistic activities of the converted Saul would get him in trouble with, you guessed it, the Jews.

Saul escaped Damascus and ended up in Jerusalem. But there was one small problem: the disciples didn't trust Saul. After all, previously Saul had been trying to put Christians in jail, and now he was claiming to be one of them! Seems a little fishy to me too. Cue the flashy theme music. Enter the mentor! "But Barnabas took him and brought him to the apostles and declared to them how on the road he had seen the Lord, who spoke to him, and how at Damascus he had preached boldly in the name of Jesus" (Acts 9:27). And so, a mentoring relationship began between Paul and Barnabas under the most trying circumstances.

---

49 The full story of Saul's conversion and following evangelistic activity is found in Acts 9:1–25.

A STAR IS BORN

Just like that, Saul of Tarsus, under the mentoring relationship of Barnabas, became an evangelistic rock star. But not so fast! Mentoring takes time and patience. After all, this is a relationship, and relationships need time: time to grow, experience ups and downs, celebrate successes, and ultimately, pass the baton from the mentor to the mentee so that the gifts and knowledge may pass on to future generations.

Hollywood has a fascination (and, dare I say, love affair) with the mentor-mentee relationship. In the years 1937, 1954, 1976, and 2018, moviegoers were treated to the cinematic spectacular *A Star Is Born.* Each production is slightly different from the others, but the basic story line remains the same. *A Star Is Born* is part romance, part tragedy. The story follows a dynamic and talented young woman in a rags-to-riches climb. In all four presentations of the movie, the plot follows a similar trajectory: An aging male celebrity who is riddled by addictions meets a talented and younger woman with whom he is instantly smitten. He is attuned to her overwhelming talent and mentors her career. Before you know it, she is a star. Meanwhile, his career sinks deeper and deeper into the doldrums.

The most recent rendition of *A Star Is Born* was brought to the big screen in 2018 by director and actor Bradley Cooper, who plays the lead, Jackson Maine, and his costar Lady Gaga, who plays the budding star Ally.[50] Jackson Maine is a country-rock singer whose career is starting the slow slide down the mountain.

---

50 *A Star Is Born*, directed by Bradley Cooper (2018; Burbank, CA: Warner Brothers Home Entertainment, 2019), DVD.

After a concert, he goes to a bar, where Ally is on stage singing. At once, Jackson is overwhelmed with the beauty and power of her voice as well as her physical beauty. He is compelled to meet her, to be in her presence. He wants to understand this talent and foster it along. He is persistent. Ally is self-critical—of her talent, of her beauty, of her voice. And then the mentor relationship is born. Jackson tells Ally: "Look, talent comes everywhere. . . . But having something to say and a way to say it so people listen to it, that's a whole other bag. And unless you get out there and you try to do it, you'll never know. That's just the truth."[51]

The mentor is persistent and affirming. Jackson will not let Ally wallow in self-defeat, nor will he let her paralyze herself and her career with self-criticism. She has talent and something to say to the world, and the world needs to hear it. In a similar way, Barnabas came alongside Saul and was persistent and affirming: "But Barnabas took him and brought him to the apostles and declared to them how on the road he had seen the Lord, who spoke to him, and how at Damascus he had preached boldly in the name of Jesus" (Acts 9:27).

Saul had something to say, and the world needed to hear it. And what was it that Saul had to say? We are told in the Book of Acts that in the days following his conversion, Saul spent time with the disciples in Damascus, "and immediately he proclaimed Jesus in the synagogues, saying, 'He is the Son of God'" (Acts 9:20). Saul was preaching boldly in the name of Jesus. However, what we don't want to miss is that Saul spent time with those wiser and more mature in the faith—the disciples in Damascus. He grew in his understanding and walk of faith. And when Saul

---

51 To view this scene, watch from 8:03 to 21:35 (scenes 2–3).

arrived in Jerusalem, Barnabas came alongside him and continued to assist him in his walk of faith. Saul was not left on his own to figure things out. Saul was being mentored.

We, too, have something to say when it comes to matters of faith. Like Saul, we know Jesus Christ to be the Son of God. However, our understanding of the Gospel needs to grow and mature. This is done best when we have mentors in the faith who come alongside us and help us to understand the revelation of sacred Scripture. Faithful pastors and teachers help us grow in our understanding and spiritual maturity. Like Saul, we need disciples in Damascus and a Barnabas to help us with our confession and expression of faith as we share what is most important with those around us. Like Ally, we need a Jackson to be persistent in prodding us to sing our song of faith while affirming our ability to do so.

STANDING ON STAGE TOGETHER

Mentors do not demand the spotlight. Although the light shines brightly upon them, this is not their primary goal. Mentors look to share the light, spread the light, and bring others into the light with them. Mentors coach and assist, challenge and direct, push and prod. The mentor is willing to bring others onto the big stage of life and celebrate their skills and successes with them.

The dynamic between Jackson Maine and Ally in *A Star Is Born* wonderfully demonstrates the humility of a mentoring relationship. When Jackson leaves Ally for a performance far away, he sends a limousine to fetch Ally and bring her to the venue. Why? Although Jackson is a big star who performs at sold-out venues, he not only is willing to sing a song written by Ally but also wants her to be on the stage with him. After all, it is her song and her words. She has something to say, and the world needs to hear it.

He is the conduit by which that voice has a stage, a platform to be heard by the masses. In a tender and warm moment, after performing one of his hits, he slows down the music and begins to play the song Ally wrote. Ally, standing off-stage, is in shock: her song, her words, being performed for the masses. And then Jackson gives her a look—a gentle nod—to join him on the stage. He invites her to sing her song, to share her words, to let the world hear her voice. And Ally sings out. She sings loud. She sings with joy and emotion. The crowd responds favorably to her voice and her song. And the mentor, Jackson, smiles and laughs. Her success is his success.[52]

But this is not a one-and-done proposition. Personal growth comes from practice and experience. Jackson knows Ally needs to be on the stage. She needs to learn what it means to command a stage as a performer. She needs the accolades of singing songs the audience knows as well as to introduce her songs to the same people. The mentor, Jackson, knows that this is a process, and he is Ally's guide through it. *A Star Is Born* takes us on a journey of Ally finding her voice and sharing her music while Jackson basks in the glow of a mentee moving beyond the mentor.[53]

What Jackson does for Ally is not a Hollywood invention. Mentors know that their mentees must come out from behind the curtain to the center of the stage in order to grow. Mentors know that the individuals need to experience everything that comes

---

52 To view this scene, watch from 38:25 to 42:05 (scene 7).

53 Scenes 8 through 10 take the audience on a journey of the mentor-mentee relationship. As Ally increases in skill and confidence, Jackson continues to unravel. Although he has great joy in her success, his own life is exposed to her for its conflict, pain, and hardship. Consider watching from 38:25 to 1:07:03 (scenes 8–10).

from being in the light. Head knowledge and personal skills need to be tested and challenged. Heart knowledge needs to be shared. Faith needs to be expressed. Songs need to be sung.

In the early days of the Christian Church, Christians scattered after the persecution of Stephen. Many believers traveled as far from Jerusalem as Phoenicia, Cyprus, and Antioch. When they arrived, they began to share the message of Jesus with the Jews. "But there were some of them, men of Cyprus and Cyrene, who on coming to Antioch spoke to the Hellenists also, preaching the Lord Jesus" (Acts 11:20). The Gospel needed to be proclaimed. The song of salvation needed to be sung, not only to the Hebrews but also to the Hellenists. Hellenists? What is a Hellenist? Hellenists were Greek-speaking Jews of the diaspora. This was the first large-scale dipping of the toe in different cultural waters with the Gospel, where the potential recipients weren't exactly like them. The Bible tells us, "The hand of the Lord was with them, and a great number who believed turned to the Lord" (Acts 11:21).

What does this have to do with mentoring relationships? The story continues: "The report of this came to the ears of the church in Jerusalem, and they sent Barnabas to Antioch" (Acts 11:22). Think back to Acts 4:36. Barnabas was a Cypriot Jew. Sending him to Antioch made sense. After all, he was from that neck of the woods. This was a moment for Barnabas to shine! Here was his moment to be Jackson Maine on the center stage of evangelistic activity. And shine he did: "When he came and saw the grace of God, he was glad, and he exhorted them all to remain faithful to the Lord with steadfast purpose, for he was a good man, full of the Holy Spirit and of faith. And a great many people were added to the Lord" (Acts 11:23–24).

But mentors need to mentor, and that's what Barnabas did! Barnabas knew the song of the Gospel needed to be sung and that Saul needed to sing it with him: "So Barnabas went to Tarsus to look for Saul, and when he had found him, he brought him to Antioch. For a whole year they met with the church and taught a great many people. And in Antioch the disciples were first called Christians" (Acts 11:25–26). Did you catch that? Barnabas went to Tarsus to find Saul. Barnabas was willing to travel about 150 miles each way to get Saul and bring him back to Antioch to further his mentoring. That is how important the mentoring relationship was to Barnabas. Barnabas knew the evangelistic zeal of Saul. Barnabas knew the potential of Saul's ministry. And Barnabas was willing to share the spotlight with him.

Barnabas and Saul worked closely together for a year. They met with people, shared their faith, and grew together as brothers in Christ. Barnabas invested time into the relationship, walking closely with Saul as he grew in confidence, knowledge, and conviction. Saul had something to say about Jesus, and people needed to listen to it. Barnabas knew that Saul had to share that message. By the end of that year, the mentor and the mentee had grown exponentially in faith and in friendship.

For the first time, Saul was recognized as a leader alongside Barnabas. He was coming out of the shadow of the mentor. When Agabus (a prophet) foretold a famine that would come over the world, the Church responded. "So the disciples determined, every one according to his ability, to send relief to the brothers living in Judea. And they did so, sending it to the elders by the hand of Barnabas and Saul" (Acts 11:29–30). Barnabas and Saul, linked together. Mentor and mentee. Teacher and student. Pastor and vicar. Saul was growing, and I suspect that Barnabas smiled and laughed like Jackson Maine, that he was filled with joy. What else would a mentor do? Saul grew rapidly and became a leader among the people. The mentor's work was producing fruit for the kingdom of God.

The Christian mentor is critical in the walk of faith. Like Saul, we need a Barnabas who is willing to go to great lengths to help foster our faith and witness. We need faith-filled people who are mature in their Christian walk to invest time, energy, and effort in our lives to help us grow and realize our full capacity and expression of evangelistic zeal in a lost and dying world. Not only did Barnabas travel to great lengths to find Saul, but he then also invested a full year of mentoring and prodding to produce the very best from Saul. I am sure that if you look back over your course of faith and life, you have a Barnabas or two who have come alongside you and who were willing to go the extra mile, spend the extra hours, and invite you onto the stage of faithfulness to let the Gospel light shine. Like Ally, you may be overwhelmed by their investment in you! For the spiritually mature readers, I bet there are a few Sauls in your life whom you have served like Barnabas. You are probably smiling as you think about how their bright and vibrant faith captivated the stage, the song of the Gospel they sang, the message they proclaimed! Like Jackson Maine, you are smiling and laughing!

SUCCESS AND FAILURE AND SUCCESS

Unfortunately, Hollywood tends to paint a picture of mentorship that is dramatic and heart-wrenching but not necessarily realistic. You see, mentors and those they mentor may not always be on the same page. The tension can escalate when the mentee begins to move beyond the tutelage provided by the mentor. Careers can take off while the knowledge and experience of the mentee expand. The mentor may still have a great deal of wisdom and insight to offer, even as the mentee begins to advance and soar, but the mentee feels ready to explore his or her newfound skills apart from the mentor. The mentee may begin to believe that he or she knows better than the mentor.

In many respects, this is what happens in *A Star Is Born*. The mentor and the mentee are cascading toward crisis. They are deeply in love, but Ally's career is beginning to soar to new heights, while Jackson is left behind. In true Hollywood style, Jackson and Ally marry, but it's not enough to bridge the widening professional gap that is forming between the two. Competing voices are now trying to direct and map out Ally's blossoming career. Meanwhile, Jackson is spiraling downward as he becomes more intertwined with the demons of chemical dependency.

Even during these increasing challenges, Jackson Maine is still mentoring, still helping, still loving Ally. Ally is about to launch her career down a very different path than Jackson anticipated, so he takes her out onto a balcony to talk with her alone. A billboard with Ally's face and name looms behind them. In this tender and sincere moment, Jackson offers his last and most profound mentoring words. He tells Ally, "All you got is you and what you want to say to people. And they are listening right now, and they're not gonna be listening forever."[54]

In these simple yet profound words, Jackson reminds Ally to be honest to herself. He challenges her to be true to her voice, her words, and her passion. He reminds her that people love the

---

54 To view this scene, watch from 1:20:13 to 1:20:30 (scene 13).

songs of her heart. It's not about the glamour and the money, the stylists and designers, the agents and the albums. It is about a song from the heart, and people are listening. How does Jackson know this? Because he has traveled this road. The mentor knows because he has been there himself. Jackson knows because people have listened to him—to his songs—and he knows what it's like when they stop listening. He possesses the priceless commodity of experience, and he wants to share that with Ally so that she doesn't make the same mistakes. The mentor wants the very best for the mentee; Jackson wants the very best for Ally.

Barnabas and Saul—now called Paul[55]—seemed to be on a similar trajectory. They had become effective and prolific missionaries for the Christian Church. What is often called Paul's first missionary journey was actually undertaken by both Paul and his mentor, Barnabas. Leaving from Antioch in Syria, the two journeyed to Seleucia, Cyprus, Salamis, Paphos, Perga, Antioch in Pisidia, Iconium, Lystra, Derbe, and Attalia before returning to Antioch in Syria.[56] Like Jackson Maine and Ally on a concert tour, these two missionaries for the Gospel were traveling together, proclaiming God's Word together, and finding success as people wanted to hear what they had to say. People wanted to hear the Gospel of Jesus Christ.

Barnabas and Paul were at the apex of their brotherly missionary activity. By all appearances, nothing could stop them. The world needed to hear about Jesus, and they were ready to go. But conflict and disagreement often lurk around the corners of success and gain. Distractions and competing voices always seem

---

55 In Acts 13:9, Saul is called "Paul" for the first time on the island of Cyprus. The author of Acts indicates that the names were interchangeable.

56 You can follow their journey in Acts 13–14.

to tug people in opposite directions. Look at what happened to Barnabas and Paul:

> And after some days Paul said to Barnabas, "Let us return and visit the brothers in every city where we proclaimed the word of the Lord, and see how they are." Now Barnabas wanted to take with them John called Mark. But Paul thought best not to take with them one who had withdrawn from them in Pamphylia and had not gone with them to the work. And there arose a sharp disagreement, so that they separated from each other. Barnabas took Mark with him and sailed away to Cyprus, but Paul chose Silas and departed, having been commended by the brothers to the grace of the Lord. And he went through Syria and Cilicia, strengthening the churches. (ACTS 15:36–41)

A "sharp disagreement" arose between Barnabas and Paul over whether John Mark should join them on this journey. So what happened?

A quick look back to the first missionary journey in Acts 13–14 is quite revealing. John Mark was with Barnabas and Paul—that is, until they arrived in Perga. When they were in Perga, the account simply states, "And John [Mark] left them and returned to Jerusalem" (Acts 13:13). Why did John Mark leave? That is a question for biblical scholars to debate.[57] But we do know this: it

---

57 In his commentary on Acts, F. F. Bruce writes this: "Paul regarded his [John Mark's] departure as desertion. Perhaps he was unprepared for the increasing rigors which evangelization in Asia Minor would involve; perhaps he resented the way in which his cousin Barnabas was falling into second place. When the expedition sets out from Syria, Luke speaks of 'Barnabas and Saul'; by the time they leave Cyprus, it is 'Paul and his company.' It is unlikely that this change of expression is due purely to a change of source." F. F. Bruce, *The Book of Acts*, The New International Commentary on the New Testament (Grand Rapids: Eerdmans, 1988), 251.

did not sit well with Paul. And John Mark was Barnabas's cousin! Thus, the mentor and the mentee reached the crossroads. There was disagreement and heartache. Heels were dug in and lines were drawn. The mentor-mentee relationship between Barnabas and Paul was fractured. To further complicate the matter, Paul and Barnabas went their separate ways. We are told that Barnabas took Mark along with him and set sail for Cyprus. Paul, on the other hand, invited Silas to join him, and they visited the churches in Syria and Cilicia. Barnabas got in a boat; Paul went the other direction by land.

Friction can serve as a catalyst. By bumping into obstacles and opposing points of view, we are forced to find a way forward. In the case of Barnabas and Paul, the friction they experienced in Antioch furthered the advancement of the Gospel by doubling their efforts to visit new Christian congregations and share the Gospel—Barnabas and John Mark to Cyprus, and Paul and Silas to Syria and Cilicia. Paul, the mentee, was ready for this moment to step out on his own and engage the mission field without the watchful eye of Barnabas. Barnabas had coached Paul and helped him grow into an effective witness and evangelist for the Church of Jesus Christ. And then Barnabas did what mentors do: he took John Mark under his wing and went off to Cyprus to build up young believers and continue to share the Gospel with new people. Although this is not how we would want the story to end with Barnabas (he is not mentioned in the Book of Acts again), by no means was his story over.

Hollywood loves the dramatic. When the mentor has nothing left to give, when the mentor has imparted all of his or her knowledge, when the mentee has grown beyond the mentor—then the mentor has to go. In the movie *A Star Is Born*, Jackson Maine has nothing left to give. Consumed by his demons and addictions, he believes it is better to remove himself from Ally's life than to drag her down with him. And so he dies by his own hand in what he perceives to be a sacrifice of love and a gift of freedom for Ally.[58] The audience sheds tears and mourns the loss of love, but the mentee is free from the bonds of the relationship and now can embrace the spotlight that was always waiting for her in the end. A star is truly born.

Stop the music, and don't let the credits roll on this scene quite yet! Jackson Maine is dead, and Ally is left trying to figure out her life and career with her mentor gone forever. That's Hollywood! But that is not real life. Let's get back to Paul and Barnabas. Although Barnabas is not mentioned again in the Book of Acts, he is certainly not gone or forgotten in the life of Paul or in the pages of Scripture. The Book of Acts turns its attention to Paul and his mission activities. We do not have any record of Barnabas and his mission travels and further mentoring work with other new Christians. But that doesn't mean he wasn't busy or that Paul forgot about his old mentoring friend.

While Paul was busy spreading the Gospel and being an evangelistic star, Barnabas was still hard at work. How do we know? Because Paul mentioned Barnabas in some of his epistles. Paul remembered his mentor and referenced him in a spirit of cooperation and oneness in the ministry of the Gospel. Paul wrote to the Church at Corinth: "This is my defense to those who would examine me. Do we not have the right to eat and drink? Do we not have the right to take along a believing wife, as do the other apostles and the brothers of the Lord and Cephas? Or is it only

58 To view this scene, watch from 1:50:53 to 2:01:20 (scene 17).

Barnabas and I who have no right to refrain from working for a living?" (1 Corinthians 9:3–6).

Did you catch that? "Barnabas and I." A brotherly connection in Jesus. No longer mentor and mentee but co-workers in the Gospel. Were they restored as friends from their conflict from years ago? There is simply not enough in Scripture for us to be sure. But consider what Paul says to the Church in Colossae: "Aristarchus my fellow prisoner greets you, and Mark the cousin of Barnabas (concerning whom you have received instructions—if he comes to you, welcome him)" (Colossians 4:10). If John Mark was the cause of the sharp disagreement that separated Barnabas and Paul, then it appears from this verse that all was forgiven.

The point is simple: God provides us with relationships to help us grow in faith and develop our God-given talents. These individuals come alongside us and offer their experience, wisdom, knowledge, care, encouragement—along with a host of other things—so that we can grow and mature in our faith and life. Some of those mentors will help us with education, careers, life decisions, and relationships. Other mentors will help nurture and mature our faith in Jesus Christ. Not all of our mentors are fragile, broken, and addicted like Jackson Maine, stars flickering out whose only way to reconcile with our growth is to remove themselves from our lives.

Instead, most of our mentors are everyday people doing ordinary jobs—teachers, coaches, pastors, neighbors, co-workers, and friends. We meet them in our schools, neighborhoods, churches, and workplaces. They have names like Mary Ann and Robert (remember, my two mentors). And these people are critically important in our journey through this life. They give, and we receive. They love, and we embrace. We grow, and they cheer. We move on, and they stay behind, ready to mentor another. In *A Star Is Born*, chance brought Jackson into a mentoring relationship with Ally. But it wasn't by chance that Barnabas came alongside Saul (or Paul), and it isn't by chance your mentors have come alongside you. Mentoring relationships will always have success stories and failures, ups and downs. The key is recognizing these amazing people for who they are: gifts of God to us!

Discussion Questions

1. What is a mentor? What do mentors do? Where do you find mentors in the world today?

2. Whom do you consider to be your mentors? How did you meet them? What specific role did they play in your life?

3. Read Acts 4:36–37. What qualities or characteristics stand out regarding Joseph, who was called Barnabas? Why was the name *Barnabas* appropriate for this man?

4. Read Acts 9:26–31. How does Barnabas enter into a mentoring relationship with Saul? What was he willing to do or say on Saul's behalf? How does a mentor stand up for the mentee?

5. In the movie *A Star Is Born*, Jackson Maine serves as a mentor to Ally. Early in the movie, Jackson is affirming and persistent in nurturing her career. How does Barnabas nurture Saul in his witness and evangelism? How has someone mentored your faith in Jesus?

6. Jackson and Ally shared a stage just like Barnabas and Saul shared a pulpit. How does the Church nurture leaders today? Cite examples of mentoring relationships that share responsibilities in the ministry.

7. In *A Star Is Born*, the mentor takes his own life in order for the mentee's career to advance. When a mentor-mentee relationship ends, how does the possible friction offer opportunity? Read Acts 15:36–41. What good came out of the sharp disagreement between Barnabas and Paul? Do you still have a relationship with your mentor(s)? If so, what kind? If not, why not?

8. What challenged you in this scene? What did you find affirming to your faith?

TICKET
THE END
CINEMA
MOVIE
TICKET
THE END

SCENE 7

THE MANY FACETS OF LOVE

FEATURE PRESENTATION

THE PRINCESS BRIDE

Do you remember your first love? Maybe you are one of the rare few who never parted ways with your first love—you got married and are still together to this day. But if you are like most, your first love remains tucked away somewhere in the pages of a high school yearbook or deep in the recesses of your mind. And you are comfortable with that. It is a distant memory about which you can reminisce through rose-colored glasses. That person is perfectly preserved in teenage beauty and unhardened by the advancement of time.

All of that came crashing down with the creation of social media. Suddenly, first loves and other people from your deep and distant past are knocking at your social-media door. Friend requests populate your app, and you feel trapped! To accept or ignore—that is the question! But let's face facts: We are not all wired the same. Some of us can easily ignore that ominous friend request. You are strong, your life has moved on, and that person needs to remain in the past. There is simply no room in the current context of your life for this person to reappear. With the tap of your finger, that person is ignored and removed from your life once again.

However, many people are not that strong. In fact, they are a little more than curious about their past love. Where has life taken this person? Are they as beautiful as I remember? Did he or she get married and have children? And of course, maybe the biggest question of all: why is this person sending me a friend request now? Your finger hovers between *accept* and *ignore*, a very real emotional challenge!

NOT ALL FRIEND REQUESTS ARE EQUAL

Take a moment and look at your past. Who might come knocking on your social-media door? Not every friend request from your past will be a former romantic interest! In fact, many of those requests will be from people who were once an important part of your life. As you journey through life, all sorts of people walk with you for a period of time. Some will travel short distances with you and then fade away. Others will journey with you for a long time, and then circumstances will cause you to go in different directions. Some of these relationships are romantic, while others are marked by deep and abiding friendship. Some will be remembered as turbulent and tumultuous; others will bring a great sense of peace and joy.

Thanks to the internet and all the social-media outlets at our disposal, this wide and varied tapestry of people from our past can come looking for us. I am sure you have had your moments when a person from your past sent you a friend request, much to your angst and chagrin. You had moved on and away from that person for a reason. And now here is that person, knocking at your door once again. But I'm also sure you have received a friend request that warmed your heart because it brought back a flood of good memories and friendship from long ago. You miss that person being in your life. He or she was your friend in all the best expressions of that word.

LOVE

If you were to stop and consider what held all of these once-upon-a-time relationships together, you would ultimately land on the word *love.* In all of its many facets, love is what brought you together for that time and in that place. Love defined your romantic feelings, friendship, and joy; love defined your relationship with those people. And when the relationship ended—by choice, decision, or design—love was fractured.

We are in love with the word *love.* It seems to find its way into everything, from movies to music to books to conversations. Take music, for example. During the 1980s, the word *love* was one of the five most frequently used words in pop music.[59] Go back a generation and consider the Beatles. During their musical tidal wave during the 1960s, they used the word *love* in 11 song titles and 613 times within the lyrics of their entire catalog of songs. That's a lot!

Love is a broad word. It runs the gamut of expression and application, including people and things. For example, you can love pizza and also love your children; you can love traveling and love your friend; you can love your spouse and you can also love a movie. *Love* seems so simple to define, yet it is profoundly complex because of the vast terrain it is forced to cover in our language.

---

59 Paul Zollo, "The Most Popular Words in American Popular Songs," *American Songwriter*, July 2020, https://americansongwriter.com/popular-words-in-popular-songs/.

WE NEED MORE

The English language doesn't do love justice. Four letters are simply not enough! We need more—more letters, or better yet, more words! The ancient Greeks would agree. In the Greek language, one word did not express all the nuances that are lumped into this one English word. Instead, the Greeks assigned a different word for each facet of love. The ancient Greeks had at least six different words to describe love. Romantic, friendship, affectionate, familial, even self-love—the Greeks took the business of love to a whole new level!

Although I love words and language, I think even I would have a hard time remembering so many different words for our lonely English word *love*! Maybe we need to simplify and find a happy medium between the Greek and English languages when it comes to love. You probably know that the Bible was not originally written in English. It was written in Hebrew and Greek. And to complicate matters, somewhere between the third and first centuries BC, the Hebrew Old Testament was translated into Greek (this translation is called the Septuagint). Let's take a quick look at what words the translators of the Old Testament and the writers of the New Testament used for *love* and how they used these words to express its many facets.

FOUR BIBLICAL LOVES

The first biblical love is *eros*. This is the Greek word that is used to describe romantic or sensual love. This kind of love seeks its own satisfaction and fulfillment. But *eros* can be a two-edged sword.

It can be a beautiful expression of love when demonstrated in the bond of marriage, such as in these verses from the Song of Solomon: "Let him kiss me with the kisses of his mouth! For your love is better than wine; your anointing oils are fragrant; your name is oil poured out; therefore virgins love you. Draw me after you; let us run. The king has brought me into his chambers" (1:2–4). But *eros* can also lead a person astray. This is why the Letter to the Hebrews warns us: "Let marriage be held in honor among all, and let the marriage bed be undefiled, for God will judge the sexually immoral and adulterous" (Hebrews 13:4). *Eros* can be beautiful when expressed between a husband and wife. However, it is toxic when expressed selfishly and recklessly.

The second biblical love is *storge*. This Greek word describes the affectionate bond between family members—parents and children, brothers and sisters. We see this kind of familial love all over the Old Testament. Abraham and Sarah express this *storge* with their son, Isaac, and who can forget Jacob and his *storge* for his sons (especially Joseph!). How about in the New Testament? An expression of *storge* can be seen in the mother of James and John when she comes to Jesus and makes the big ask regarding the seats on Jesus' right and left in His kingdom (Matthew 20:20–21). She wanted the very best for her sons because of her *storge* for them. *Storge* can transcend the biological connection of family. The apostle Paul applies *storge* to the Christian community: "Love one another with brotherly affection. Outdo one another in showing honor" (Romans 12:10). In other words, within the Church, love one another like a family, because you are a family!

The third biblical love is *philia.* This Greek word expresses deep and abiding friendship. Words such as *beloved*, *dear*, and *confidant* come to mind for this kind of love. Jesus expressed *philia* when He said, "This is My commandment, that you love one another as I have loved you. Greater love has no one than this, that someone lay down his life for his friends. You are My friends if you do what I command you" (John 15:12–14). With *philia*, people cherish their friends and cannot conceive of life without these people in it. Friendship and *philia* are inseparable.

The fourth biblical love is *agape*. This kind of love is selfless, sacrificial, perfect, and pure. *Agape* is the pinnacle of the love mountain! It transcends human relationships and expresses the divine. The Gospel of John captures the totality of *agape*: "For God so loved the world, that He gave His only Son, that whoever believes in Him should not perish but have eternal life" (John 3:16). God gave Himself *to* us and *for* us.

But God also expects us to express *agape*. How? Later in the Gospel of John, the resurrected Jesus appeared to His disciples along the shore. Jesus asked Peter three times: "Simon, son of John, do you love Me?" The first two times Jesus asked this question, He used the word *agape*. Both times, Peter shrank back, knowing he could not generate that sacrificial love by himself, likely remembering his failures in the hours leading up to Jesus' crucifixion. He answered that he loved Jesus with *philia*. The third time, Jesus used the word *philia*. In these verses of epic restoration, Jesus loved Peter and called upon him to express reciprocal love. On his own, Peter could never generate that *agape* love. But in repentance, Peter could now be filled with the Holy Spirit, who in turn filled him with the *agape* love that would move him to risk his safety and eventually his life for the Gospel of Jesus. Selfless, sacrificial, perfect, and pure love is the ultimate expression of faith. *Agape* love is embodied in Jesus and is reflected in the believer back to God. *Agape* is faith in action!

THAT'S A WHOLE LOT OF LOVE

By now you might be thinking to yourself, "That's a whole lot of love!" And it is. Just trying to discern and decipher if I'm receiving or giving love can be hard enough, so to consider what *kind* of love I'm engaged in is a whole other challenge. In 1987, director Rob Reiner and 20th Century Fox released the movie *The Princess Bride.* Adapted from William Goldman's 1973 novel of the same name, the movie tells the story of a farm boy named Westley (played by Cary Elwes) who, with the help of some friends he picks up along the way, seeks to rescue his one true love, Princess Buttercup (played by Robin Wright), from the diabolical clutches of Prince Humperdinck (played by Chris Sarandon). But along Westley's journey, we see the many facets of love played out on the big screen.[60]

The movie begins with a young boy (played by Fred Savage) sick at home. His mother informs him that his grandfather (played by Peter Falk) has come over for a visit. The boy exclaims to his mother, "Can't you tell him I'm sick?" He wants to play his video game, and he doesn't want his cheek pinched! Much to his chagrin, his mother replies, "That's why he's here." The grandfather walks into the room, pinches the boy's cheek, sits himself down in a chair, and gives the boy a present. Who doesn't love a present when they are sick in bed! But when the boy tears off the wrapping paper, it's just an old, well-worn, well-loved book. The boy's disappointment is palpable. However, the grandfather is relentless. He tells the boy that this was the book his father read to him when he was sick

---

60 *The Princess Bride*, directed by Rob Reiner (1987; Santa Monica, CA: MGM Home Entertainment, 2001), DVD.

and the same book he read to the boy's father when he was sick. Now he is going to share this book with his grandson.[61]

Although *The Princess Bride* will unfold into a fun and frolicking tale with fairy-tale characters, the story is framed by this family relationship. The heart and soul of this movie is about a grandfather who loves his grandson. But what kind of love? When separating the fantasy from the reality, we realize that the love played out in this sick boy's room is *storge*: the affectionate bond between a grandfather and a grandson. The grandfather is there because he loves his grandson and wants to help him feel better. He wants to bring joy and happiness to this child. And the grandfather knows a little secret: the book he brought for his grandson will reveal the many facets of love to his grandson. The grandfather reading this book to his grandson will soon reveal to the child the *storge*—the love—that is sitting in the chair next to his bed.

When we reflect upon our families, our mothers and fathers, sisters and brothers, grandmothers and grandfathers, we can be filled with a flood of emotions. Families are not perfect—far from it! But more often than not, we are filled with a sense of love for our families. We want them to be safe and secure. We want them to be free of pain, suffering, anguish, and anger. Consider God's servant Noah. The world had grown desperate, filled with violence and corruption. That's when God came calling on Noah and instructed him to build the ark. The ark was big—really, really big! It would be a massive undertaking. And how about all of the animals? What would compel Noah to do all of this under the critical eye of neighbors and friends? What would motivate Noah to finish this project despite ridicule and judgment?

---

61 To view this scene, watch from 00:00 to 2:16 (scene 1, "Main Title/Grandpa Visit").

God tells Noah:

> For behold, I will bring a flood of waters upon the earth to destroy all flesh in which is the breath of life under heaven. Everything that is on the earth shall die. But I will establish My covenant with you, and you shall come into the ark, you, your sons, your wife, and your sons' wives with you. (GENESIS 6:17–18)

In a word: family. Noah was a faithful servant of the Lord. He did as the Lord instructed him. In fact, he did as the Lord instructed him without question. But let's not overlook what God told Noah: Bring your wife and your sons and your daughters-in-law! The ark was more than a vessel to protect the animals and repopulate the earth. The ark was the vehicle by which Noah's family would be protected and blessed. Building the big boat on dry land was an undertaking of *storge* for his family. Noah loved them. And the ark was a part of God's plan to provide for and protect Noah's family.

To what lengths would you go to provide for and protect your family? What sacrifices are you willing to make so your children have what they need? What sacrifices would you make for your parents, or for a brother or sister? Love like this binds family together. The familial love of *storge* means we will go to great lengths to protect, provide for, and care for those within our family group. Like the grandfather reading a special book to his grandson in *The Princess Bride*, we also have family traditions and special experiences with our loved ones. Treasure these moments with your family. Why? Because the floodwaters will come, life can be painfully unpredictable, and our days are numbered on this side of eternity. These moments are gifts of God through which we can experience the *storge* we share with our family.

IS THIS A KISSING BOOK?

As the grandfather begins to read the book to his sick grandson, the audience is taken from the boy's bedroom to a far-off land. We are brought to a simple and humble farm. The story is coming to life! The audience hears the grandfather narrating while Westley and Buttercup act out the story. A handsome farm boy and a beautiful girl. The dance of flirtation has begun. Every time Buttercup asks Westley to do something, he answers her with the simple words "As you wish." With each simple task he is asked to do, the words he speaks remain constant and true: "As you wish." The narrator then tells us that every time Westley says, "As you wish," he is really saying, "I love you." And what is amazing is that one day Buttercup realizes she loves Westley back.

But Westley is poor and wants to provide. He leaves the farm in search of fortune and fame. Buttercup is left worrying that she will never see Westley again. Westley has told Buttercup that what they have is true love, that regardless where his travels take him, he will come back and seek her out. True love cannot be defeated![62] However, at this point in their relationship, true love may not be what we see playing out on the screen. In fact, as we consider the types of love, it is pretty clear that Westley and Buttercup are engaged in the dance of *eros*. The love they share is romantic and sensual. As the sick grandson listens to his grandfather read, he figures this out very quickly! He asks his grandfather suspiciously, "Wait a minute! . . . Is this a *kissing* book?"

Eros is a gift of God to His children. Beauty, sensuality, and personal attraction are all a part of the love connection.

62 To view this scene, watch from 2:15 to 5:44 (scene 2, "A Kissing Book").

Don't believe me? Just take a look at the Song of Solomon in the Old Testament. It is one of the most sensual, descriptive, and captivating books about love—the *eros* kind of love! And this love is not a one-way street. It is expressed by both the man and the woman. For example, the bride confesses, "Let him kiss me with the kisses of his mouth! For your love is better than wine; your anointing oils are fragrant; your name is oil poured out; therefore virgins love you" (Song of Solomon 1:2–3). And what about the groom? "You are beautiful, my love; behold, you are beautiful; your eyes are doves" (Song of Solomon 1:15). Something tells me these verses are not ordinarily found in your devotional literature!

Consider your own romantic relationships and attractions. As the saying goes, beauty is in the eye of the beholder—that is, beauty is subjective. What one person finds attractive, another person may not. And so we embark on the difficult quest to find our love connection, the person who makes our hearts beat faster and our palms get a little sweaty. We want that person who takes our breath away, and we hope we will provide him or her with the same feeling.

Maybe that's why *eros* is so difficult. It is subjective not only on our own part but also on the part of the person we desire. And so we struggle as we search for the perfect match. Dating services have turned into dating websites and apps. As we search, we still desire *eros*. We still want our hearts to beat faster and our palms to sweat. It's not just personality profiles and common interests! We want what Westley and Buttercup have in *The Princess Bride*. It is a kissing book, and we want to have a husband or wife who evokes this kind of feeling. We want this *eros* kind of love!

YOU DON'T LOOK SO GOOD. YOU DON'T SMELL SO GOOD!

Besides Westley and Buttercup, *The Princess Bride* is full of memorable, entertaining characters who teach us about other facets of love. Early in the movie, Princess Buttercup is kidnapped, and we meet two of her captors: Inigo Montoya (played by Mandy Patinkin) and Fezzik (played by Andre the Giant). The two men do not want harm to befall Buttercup. It is clear they are honorable men guided by a sense of care and compassion. It is also clear they enjoy each other's company. While aboard a ship, they play a simple rhyming game. It is innocent banter, but it is also more than that. The game demonstrates the deep and abiding friendship the two men share. Here, we see an expression of *philia*: a genuine, deep, and abiding friendship between Inigo and Fezzik.[63]

These two men care for each other. They share values and ideals. They want to support each other and help each other succeed. When one falters, the other rises up. When one is weak, the other is strong. Later in the movie, when Inigo Montoya is defeated and consumed with self-doubt and personal failing, Fezzik lifts him up. Inigo is inebriated and lost in his misery. But then Fezzik comes along and speaks words that only a friend can say in *philia*: "You don't look so good. You don't smell so good either." He says what only a friend can say to another friend (and not get punched in the face). These are not words of judgment; they are words of *philia* and concern. Fezzik nurses his inebriated friend back to health. He enlivens his spirit and stands by him in his hour

---

63 To view this scene, watch from 7:26 to 10:00 (scene 4, "Three Circus Performers").

of need. They are ready for the adventure ahead because they are together, and nothing can stop their brotherly love![64]

Have you ever stopped to consider that Jesus had friends? I'm not talking about the twelve disciples, although they were most certainly His friends too! Jesus had other friends whom He loved and cherished, who were important and close to Him. Jesus had a deep and abiding friendship with two sisters and a brother: Mary, Martha, and Lazarus. The Gospel of John states, "Now Jesus loved Martha and her sister and Lazarus" (John 11:5). And if that were not enough, Jesus, upon learning that Lazarus had died, said, "Our friend Lazarus has fallen asleep, but I go to awaken him" (John 11:11). Jesus even hung out at their house from time to time![65] Jesus had friends, and I suspect that even as the Son of God, Jesus needed these friendships because they provided *philia*—love—as He traveled the difficult and challenging road to the cross.

During our journey through life, we need to experience *philia*. We need deep and abiding friendships. We need the voices, presence, care, and affection of trusted people who become like family. Friends have the capacity to speak truth to us even when we don't want to hear it. They can lift our spirits because they know us so well.

I have had the true joy and pleasure of having such a friend for more than twenty-five years. I cannot imagine my life without my friend Dave. He can make me laugh with a silly meme or sober my judgment with a thoughtful word. We celebrate together, mourn together, cry together, and laugh together. We pray for each other and call each other regularly—especially when life

---

64 To view this scene, watch from 1:01:00 to 1:03:44 (scene 18, "A New Alliance").

65 You can read about Jesus' friendship with Mary, Martha, and Lazarus in Luke 10:38–42; John 12:1–7.

throws challenges our way and we need each other's clarity and care to work through the dilemma. We share a common passion for playing golf, and we make sure to create space to do so even though we now live a thousand miles apart. We share *philia*, and our lives are all the richer for it.

Who are your friends? With whom do you share *philia*? Who are your Lazarus, Mary, and Martha? Who is your Fezzik, who sobers you up and is willing to tell you when you don't look or smell so good? The journey of life is a challenge all on its own. When we share *philia* with other people, we discover that the journey is not so lonely, challenging, or difficult. We discover a sense of community and belonging for which our souls hunger and thirst. We need friends! We need to give and receive *philia* just like Jesus did.

AS YOU WISH

What happens when love is so pure, tender, and all-encompassing? Would you know such love if you saw it? At the conclusion of *The Princess Bride*, the principal characters are all together: Westley, Buttercup, Inigo, and Fezzik. The many facets of love are about to be intertwined in intimate expressions of passion, family, and friendship—*eros*, *storge*, and *philia*. Westley rescues Buttercup, Inigo assists Westley, and Fezzik provides the escape to the happily ever after.[66] Love in many facets draws together in what the grandfather (who has been reading the book to his grandson the whole time) describes as "a wave of love" that swept over them.

66 To view this scene, watch from 1:27:28 to 1:33:38 (scene 27, "Bluffing").

What do you call such love? How do you describe a love that transcends friends, family, and spouse? That love is *agape*. Selfless, sacrificial, perfect, and pure. Love like this expresses what God did when He sent His Son into the world to redeem His children. *Agape* is willing to go and find the lost, rescue the imperiled, and save the endangered. It is the kind of love that puts others ahead of self.

Agape is what we are called to share and express within the context of Christian community. We are to have such love for one another as an extension and expression of the love that Jesus has for us. When such love is realized, we experience an overwhelming sense of community and belonging. We are no longer alone, lost, or loveless. We are loved by God and by our brothers and sisters in Christ. This kind of love doesn't question motive or pretense. This love means being willing to trust others in a world where deceit and peril abound. This kind of love will sacrifice and serve because we know that God first loved us. And when asked to do something, this kind of love simply says, "As you wish."

From beginning to end, *The Princess Bride* demonstrates many facets of love: a grandfather and a grandson; a farm boy and a princess; two friends working together; a group of people coming together around a common cause. When we stop and consider our own lives—moment to moment and day to day—we, too, have relationships that express the many facets of love. Even when we feel loveless and alone, we are still loved. We know that we have a God who abounds in steadfast love for us. At times, we simply need a reminder. Sometimes we need to step back, buy a movie ticket, and see it all played out on the big screen. Or better yet, we can pull out our Bible and read God's love story for us!

Discussion Questions

1. Do you remember your first love? Do you follow him or her on social media? Why or why not? Which friend requests have warmed your heart? Which friend requests have made you uncomfortable?

2. What is your favorite love song? How do you see the word *love* being used appropriately? Where do you see the word *love* being used inappropriately?

3. Name a biblical relationship that reflects *eros*. Did *eros* lead the person astray or into sin? Why or why not? How have you been challenged by *eros* in your life? Where do you see *eros* in *The Princess Bride*?

4. Name a biblical relationship that reflects *storge*. How was *storge* strengthened? How was *storge* challenged? With whom do you share *storge*? What is the *storge* relationship in *The Princess Bride*?

5. Name a biblical relationship that reflects *philia*. How did *philia* bless those who expressed it? Name a *philia* relationship you are a part of. What is the *philia* relationship in *The Princess Bride*?

6. The kind of love expressed by the Greek word *agape* is considered the pinnacle of biblical love. How did Jesus *agape* us? How are we to express *agape*? Is *agape* expressed in *The Princess Bride*? Why or why not?

7. *The Princess Bride* demonstrates various facets of love. Which type of love resonated most with you? With which characters did you find kinship? Why?

8. What challenged you in this scene? What did you find affirming to your faith?

TICKET
THE END
CINEMA
MOVIE
TICKET
THE END

ROLL THE CREDITS

In days long past, when a movie was over, it was over. The credits began to roll across the big screen, and people got up from their seats and left the theater. Nobody really seemed to care about who was the key grip or the assistant to the makeup artist. In fact, when you watch a movie at home, often the credits roll at lightning speed in a small box in the bottom corner of your screen so the next show can start. When the credits rolled, it meant the movie was over and it was time to leave the theater (or turn off the television).

However, times have changed. Now, to keep you in your seats and watch the never-ending stream of names that made this movie possible, some productions slip in a glimpse of a possible sequel or provide outtakes from scenes gone wrong during production. The rolling of the credits can be the beginning of what's next or leave you laughing with your favorite actors and actresses. If you leave too soon, you may just miss the big announcement of future movies with your favorite characters. Some movies are even so bold as to tell you, "Everyone will be back in *Such-and-Such, Volume 2*."

The movies of the Marvel Universe (owned by Disney Studios) have turned this into an art form. The studio weaves characters from one movie into another, creates new blended story lines, and then keeps you in your seat to the very last credit. You don't want to miss the hidden scene of where your favorite comic book hero will emerge next, whether that will be in a movie dedicated solely to that character or in a movie for another Marvel Universe character. The studio whets our appetites by letting us know there will be more!

How many movies have you watched for which you hoped (and, dare I say, prayed!) that a sequel would be revealed after the credits rolled? You related to the characters, loved the story line, and now you want more—more of whatever drew you to the movie in the first place. Big moments in our lives can serve in this same capacity. They are like our own big-screen moments. A big-screen moment transcends the normal and mundane and carries us to new heights, a moment that is now etched into our memories and that we visit from time to time to draw strength, encouragement, and joy. If those moments could have sequels, then sign me up!

This is why we have photo albums and digital storage to keep all of the pictures we take. It is why schools produce yearbooks and take class pictures. It is why we keep mementos from life's biggest moments and store them away in the attic, so that one day we can take the box down and rediscover those moments that were so near and dear to us. My wife and I created a box filled with such objects for each of our children. Recently, when I showed my son his box, it dawned on me that though these objects belonged to my son, they were really mine. A baptismal outfit, a first birthday candle, or a baseball uniform had no real meaning to him. After all, he was too young to remember any of it. But for me, a wash of love and joy filled my heart as I remembered with such fondness a day gone by, a day I would love to recapture in the present.

SPIRITUAL SCREENSHOT

It is important for our personal and spiritual well-being to hold on to these moments, whether we keep a picture or a memento. We don't want to forget these moments in our lives when we are blessed and our spirits filled. Jesus was quite aware of our need for this type of spiritual refreshment. In the Gospel of Matthew, Jesus took three of His disciples—Peter, James, and John—up on a mountain retreat. While they were there,

> [Jesus] was transfigured before them, and His face shone like the sun, and His clothes became white as light. And behold, there appeared to them Moses and Elijah, talking with Him. And Peter said to Jesus, "Lord, it is good that we are here. If You wish, I will make three tents here, one for You and one for Moses and one for Elijah." He was still speaking when, behold, a bright cloud overshadowed them, and a voice from the cloud said, "This is My beloved Son, with whom I am well pleased; listen to Him." When the disciples heard this, they fell on their faces and were terrified. But Jesus came and touched them, saying, "Rise, and have no fear." And when they lifted up their eyes, they saw no one but Jesus only. And as they were coming down the mountain, Jesus commanded them, "Tell no one the vision, until the Son of Man is raised from the dead." (MATTHEW 17:2–9)

The road ahead for these disciples was going to be difficult. It was a road filled with heartache and shock, persecution and perseverance, life changes and missional zeal. These disciples were blessed to be on the mountaintop with Jesus, and they knew it.

Peter exclaims, "Lord, it is good that we are here. If You wish, I will make three tents here, one for You and one for Moses and one for Elijah" (Matthew 17:4). This moment was emblazoned on their hearts and minds forever. They didn't want it to end—no, it couldn't end! But it did. And in that moment, Jesus directed them to treasure that moment amongst themselves. Later, when the road became difficult, He wanted them to share this joy-filled memory with one another and then with other people as well. Remember this moment with fondness. Revisit it as often as necessary to recapture the power, revelation, and joy of being a disciple of Jesus.

CULTURAL SCREENSHOT

Throughout this book, I hope you have been thinking about movies: movies that are important to you, movies that triggered fond memories and were followed by thoughtful conversations, movies that made you think and challenged you emotionally and intellectually. After all, movies are a form of art, and isn't that the purpose of art—to cause an emotional reaction within your very being?

But I hope that you have also come to see that movies are never created in isolation. Movies are created within the context of a culture. The language, food, social habits, norms, music, art, and sports are all a part of the creation of and participation in the cinematic experience. When you sit down in a movie theater or in front of your television, you are sitting down with all that defines your culture. You experience the movie through your cultural lenses. Sometimes, in rare moments, the movie you are watching aligns so perfectly with your cultural sensibilities that you are challenged, moved, and energized. You see and hear things differently because of it. The movie has become a part of you, a cultural expression that anchors you in the moment.

That is why I specifically chose movies from a wide variety of genres for our cinematic journey. From animation to historical fiction, superheroes to broken performers, love stories to racial equality, movies have a profound way of weaving the cultural climate into an experience that becomes relatable to you and me, the moviegoer. It is important for us to experience movies that make us uncomfortable, expand our imaginations, and make us think. Why? Because when we experience movies in such a way, we grow intellectually, morally, and spiritually.

THE MEETING POINT OF CHRIST, CULTURE, AND CINEMA

We have arrived at the convergence of Christ, culture, and cinema. Our faith in Jesus Christ defines who we are and whose we are. The apostle John says, "Beloved, we are God's children now, and what we will be has not yet appeared; but we know that when He appears we shall be like Him, because we shall see Him as He is" (1 John 3:2). When we stand under the cross of Christ and receive His gifts of love, mercy, and grace, we are the children of God.

As the children of God, we still live in the midst of our culture. We cannot avoid it or run from it. Culture is all around us. We are where God has placed us, and in that place, we are surrounded by the culture. The apostle Paul was keenly aware of the challenges we face at the intersection of Christ and culture:

> Therefore be imitators of God, as beloved children. And walk in love, as Christ loved us and gave Himself up for us,

> a fragrant offering and sacrifice to God. . . . For at one time you were darkness, but now you are light in the Lord. Walk as children of light (for the fruit of light is found in all that is good and right and true), and try to discern what is pleasing to the Lord. Take no part in the unfruitful works of darkness, but instead expose them. (EPHESIANS 5:1–2, 8–11)

Be Christlike to the culture that surrounds you. Love people wonderfully and sacrificially. Reflect the light of the Gospel to those you encounter, and illuminate the darkness of sin that pervades humankind. Interact with the culture, understand the culture, and challenge the culture with the truth that is Jesus Christ.

Then the three—Christ, culture, and cinema—converge. Cinema is the vehicle by which cultural expression finds its artistic release in a way that a wide swath of humankind can receive it. Cinema evokes a powerful personal expression. We love it or hate it. We cry, we laugh, we ponder, we get angry, and we even mourn. We are drawn to it or repelled by it. And the funny thing about cinema is that we are willing to pay to have our cultural boundaries pushed, prodded, stretched, and challenged!

As we sit in that darkened theater (or in front of our television screens), a voice echoes in our hearts and souls: the voice of faith. The voice of faith speaks into the culture played out on the big screen and says yes or no. The voice of faith sees the needs of the hurting, the wanderings of the sinful and broken, and the work of the devil who is desperately trying to keep his grasp on the culture and drag it farther from God. As we see our culture come to life at the cinema, God's Word anchors us in His eternal truth and reminds us that we are His witnesses in and to the culture.

We shed light—the light of Jesus—into the darkness of the culture as it plays out on the big screen.

The convergence is complete. Standing at the intersection of Christ, culture, and cinema are the faith-filled Christians who are called to be light and salt to the world. Jesus said to His disciples, "Go into all the world and proclaim the gospel to the whole creation" (Mark 16:15). Jesus wants His disciples—you and me—to go into the culture. He wants us to walk into the movie theaters and turn on the television screen. He didn't want us to shy away from the culture or the cinema or abandon it. He directs us to go into the culture and proclaim the Gospel. He wants us to proclaim forgiveness, love, mercy, and grace to a hurting and dying world. When we place ourselves in the midst of the culture as it is played out on the big screen, we are standing right where Jesus wants us as witnesses of His love and mercy to the whole of creation.

IT'S TIME TO LEAVE THE THEATER

Don't forget to pick up your empty popcorn bucket and place it in the trash on the way out. I always believe we should leave the theater as clean as possible so the employees don't have to clean up after our messes. You can also unsilence your cell phone. The movie is over, and we have wonderfully engaged our culture. Maybe you learned something new. Maybe you were disturbed. Or maybe, just maybe, you saw biblical images, stories, teachings, and doctrines subtly (or not so subtly!) portrayed in front of you. Whatever you saw in this movie now belongs to you. It's part of *your* cultural experience and a part of *your* spiritual journey. You stood at the convergence of Christ, culture, and cinema—and if you are like me, you can't wait to stand there again!

Discussion Questions

1. When you watch a movie, do you stay to the end of the credits? Why or why not? Have you ever been surprised by something in the final credits? What was it, and why?

2. Movies can capture big moments in our lives. What big moment in your life would you want played out on the big screen? Read Matthew 17:2–9. How did Peter want to capture the moment? What did Jesus tell the disciples to do with their experience?

3. What is your definition of art? Do you consider movies to be a form of art? Why or why not?

4. Read Ephesians 5. What does Paul instruct Christians to do regarding their interaction with the culture? How does that instruct us regarding movies?

5. How does God's Word instruct and condition how you watch a movie? Do you watch movies through biblical lenses? Why or why not?

____

____

____

6. What is your favorite genre of movie? Why? What movie do you want to watch now through Christian lenses? How do you think you will see that movie differently?

____

____

____

7. Name a movie that disappointed you. Why was it so disappointing? Where did it fail to live up to your expectations? Did you stay until the end or walk out early? Why or why not?

____

____

____

8. What movie are you excited about that has yet to be released? How do you think this book has changed how you will view this movie? What new insights into your interaction with culture have you gleaned from this book?

____

____

____

____

QUESTIONS TO PONDER WHEN YOU WATCH YOUR NEXT MOVIE

1. Why did you choose this particular movie to watch? What emotions did it evoke in you?

2. How did this movie challenge your mindset or expectations? Did the movie engage with social issues?

3. What did this movie reveal about your culture? Did it portray a culture with which you're not familiar? Was the movie's portrayal of the culture accurate? Why or why not?

4. What themes did the movie bring up? How do those themes relate to your faith?

5. What questions does this movie raise for you? How does your faith speak to those questions?

6. Are there any biblical parallels to the characters, themes, or story line of the movie?

7. How can you engage with other people based on what you learned or thought about because of this movie?

8. How was your faith challenged or affirmed by this movie? Where do you see the intersection of Christ, culture, and cinema in the movie you watched?